THE WORLD
I LEAVE YOU

ASIAN AMERICAN POETS ON
FAITH AND SPIRIT

THE WORLD
I LEAVE YOU

ASIAN AMERICAN POETS ON
FAITH AND SPIRIT

EDITED BY LEAH SILVIEUS & LEE HERRICK

The World I Leave You: Asian American Poets on Faith and Spirit
Copyright © 2020 by Lee Herrick and Leah Silvieus
For information regarding the copyright for the individual works that
appear in this volume, please consult the Acknowledgments pages
(pp. 263–271).

ISBN: 978-1-949039-05-4

Orison Books
PO Box 8385
Asheville, NC 28814
www.orisonbooks.com

Distributed to the trade by Itasca Books
1-800-901-3480 / orders@itascabooks.com
www.itascabooks.com

Cover design by Kenji C. Liu, www.kenjiliu.com
Cover image courtesy of Onlyyouqj / Freepik

Manufactured in the U.S.A.

ORISON
BOOKS

CONTENTS

WANTING TO GET CLEAR ON HER GOD-THINKING, SHE
WENT OUT INTO THAT MEADOW AGAIN:
LOCATING THE DIVINE IN THE NATURAL WORLD

WHO WILL PRAY FOR ME WHEN YOU ARE GONE?:
RELATIONSHIPS WITH CULTURAL
HISTORY AND ANCESTORS

WE WERE BROWN AND IMMIGRANT: SPIRITUAL PRACTICE AS A FORM OF POLITICAL RESISTANCE

DEAREST FATHER, FORGIVE ME FOR I HAVE SEEN:
ON DOUBT AND QUESTIONS OF FAITH

I WILL UNLOCK THE LATCH OF THESE LIPS AND PRAISE: POEMS ABOUT PRAYER AND RITUAL

INTRODUCTION

In Seoul, Korea, in the summer of 2008, Lee read from his first book *This Many Miles from Desire* at KoRoot, a guesthouse for adopted Koreans. After the reading, Leah, who was in Korea under a Fulbright teaching grant, introduced herself. There in Seoul, which was at once thousands of miles from our homes and also in the heart of the country where we were both born, Leah and Lee began a friendship in poetry that led to the book you hold in your hands. We found that we were on a similar trajectory. Adopted from South Korea to the United States, we found solace, light, and space to consider our lives and our spiritual conditions in poetry. More recently, much to our delight and surprise, through DNA testing, we discovered that we are related. This would be extraordinary enough, but for adopted Koreans who have not met close biological family, it felt like it was meant to be.

In the late summer of 2016 over a phone call that spanned both coasts as Leah stood outside a coffee shop in the rain in Brooklyn and Lee was teaching at the MFA residency at Sierra Nevada College, the journey toward this anthology began. Over the last two years, we discovered that divine connection takes many forms: discovering a good friend in poetry is a distant cousin, poetry interests aligning, and with gratitude and joy, an anthology of Asian American poets on faith and spirit, *The World I Leave You*.

According to the World Population Review, there are approximately 20 million Asian Americans in the United States, comprising 5.6 % of the country's population. Asians comprise 37% of the population in Hawaii, 14% in California, and 8-10% in New Jersey, New York, and Washington. Asian American poetry is flourishing in every corner of the country with new voices from under-represented cultures publishing exciting new work. The diaspora is vast, and the poetry of these communities reflects that vastness. We include Pacific Islanders in this anthology, as of course they are a vital part of the community. The poems here represent a small but wide-ranging sample of those voices, which exude honor, pride, and cultural exploration, among other themes. The ways in which they explore issues of faith and spirit are as diverse as the poets themselves. We hope this book will be read, taught, contemplated, questioned, and enjoyed by people from all walks of life—readers of poetry and Asian American poetry, to be sure, but we hope to engage readers of all ages, cultures, ethnicities, religions, faiths, spiritual engagements, ages, professions, political views, and literary genres.

When we issued the call for submissions, we were astonished by the immediate and enthusiastic response from poets from small towns, suburbs, and cities on both coasts and everywhere in-between, poets who represent myriad cultures, aesthetics, faiths, spiritual entry, re-entry, departure points, and belief systems. We spent two years reading, re-reading and talking about these poems. There are many more incredible poets we wanted to include, but after many conversations and deliberations, we arrived. The poems in each section contain themes that we hope place them in that section's context, but each poem could be read in another light. In other words, we invite you to use the sections as a guide but also to read and savor these poems in whatever order you desire.

The first section, "When the Sky Unhinges, How Will We Survive?: Poetry as Spiritual Witness," includes Li-Young Lee, from whose poem "Arise, Go Down" we take the evocative phrase, "The World I Leave You," as our title. This section closes with Pulitzer Prize winner Vijay Seshadri's poem, "The Long Meadow," which contemplates what it means to arrive in the next world and to realize that nothing is as one expects.

The next section, "Wanting to Get Clear on Her God-Thinking, She Went Out Into That Meadow Again: Locating the Divine in the Natural World," includes poems in which nature or the natural world play a central role. Brynn Saito contemplates the nature of divine contact, or what it means to be held by something one cannot see.

In the next section, "Who Will Pray for Me When You Are Gone?: Relationships with Cultural History and Ancestors," Khaty Xiong asks, how, in the midst of loss, in which "every evening/the car accident is the same and gives me/the same tears," we are to survive those who have passed before us—indeed, how to survive at all. Joseph O. Legaspi asks what it means to maintain our connections with our relatives and ancestors across geographical, historical, and temporal separations, and Rajiv Mohabir shows us how the songs and stories of our ancestors sustain us and create us in the midst of exile.

The next section, "We Were Brown and Immigrant: Spiritual Practice as a form of Political Resistance," includes poems that range from elegies for those who have been murdered as a result of racism, political oppression or violence to those that ask how, in the light of such devastation, as Tarfia Faizullah writes, "we gather ourselves" to resist those forces that would de-humanize us.

In the section "Dearest Father, Forgive Me For I Have Seen: On Doubt and Questions of Faith," the speaker in Ocean Vuong's "Prayer for the Newly Damned" opens and closes the poem with a question to "Dearest Father." Vuong writes," There's a boy kneeling/in a house with every door kicked open/to summer. There's a question corroding/his tongue. A knife touching/Your finger lodged inside the throat./Dearest Father, what becomes of the boy/no longer a boy? Please—what becomes of the shepherd/when the sheep are cannibals?" In Michelle Peñaloza's poem "Vestige," after the death of the speaker's Lola, Peñaloza writes, "I roll each pressed round between/my forefinger and thumb, keep count:/my guilt, my guilt, my doubt—/I am not free." In nearly all Asian American poets' lineage, there are stories of arrival and language, and whether the poets write about their elders, themselves, their future selves, or others, we see resilience and strength as much as questions and doubt. In Kaveh Akbar's poem "Despite My Efforts Even My Prayers Have Turned Into Threats," the speaker states, "My earth-/father was far braver than me—/coming to America he knew/no English save Rolling Stones/lyrics and how to say *thanks/God*."

In the final section, "I Will Unlock the Latch of These Lips and Praise: Poems About Prayer and Ritual," the poems explore the power of meditation, prayer, and ritual in relation to the divine and ineffable. Vandana Khanna contemplates the connections between prayer and the body, and the closing poem of the anthology, Mia Ayumi Malhotra's, "One Day You'll Look in the Mirror and See Lions," becomes sort of a benediction that blesses us with hope that even in the midst of the threat of violence in today's ever-changing world, that we "may not fear what lies ahead."

We are deeply grateful to the Asian American poets who came before us for the light they give us. We are deeply grateful to Kundiman, M. Evelina Galang who suggested this collaboration, Brian Turner and Christopher Buckley for editorial suggestions, and to everyone at Orison Books, in particular, founder and publisher Luke Hankins for his patience and guidance. We are deeply grateful to our families and our respective spouses, Sean and Lisa. Lastly, we are especially and deeply grateful to the remarkable poets in this anthology for their trust, their spirits, their work in the world, and their breathtaking contributions to *The World I Leave You.*

It is always the right time for faith and the spirit. It is always the right time for poetry. In a genre that is widening in wonderful, important, and inevitable ways, we offer this anthology as a contribution to the discussion, not as a defining or final word. This is merely another beginning, and we hope that this book will be an invitation that leads to many more poems, books, and ever-expanding conversations that explore the multitude of ways in which one can be Asian American, American, and spiritual or religious—and how these can provide paths to connect to our personal and collective identities, our histories, our communities, our environment, and the divine, in whatever form we experience it.

Poetry endures. Our faiths and spirits endure, too. We see our hopes for this anthology contained within its title. *The World I Leave You*: that you receive these poems as artifacts to be explored, contemplated, and savored as gifts. Thank you for reading. Thank you for your faith. Thank you for your spirit.

Leah Silvieus and Lee Herrick

New Haven, Connecticut and Fresno, California
October 2019

WHEN THE SKY UNHINGES, HOW WILL WE SURVIVE?: POETRY AS SPIRITUAL WITNESS

LI-YOUNG LEE

THE CITY IN WHICH I LOVE YOU

> "I will arise now, and go
> about the city in the streets,
> and in the broad ways I will seek…
> whom my soul loveth."
> **—Song Of Songs 3:2**

And when, in the city in which I love you,
even my most excellent song goes unanswered,
and I mount the scabbed streets,
the long shouts of avenues,
and tunnel sunken night in search of you....

That I negotiate fog, bituminous
rain ringing like teeth into the beggar's tin,
or two men jackaling a third in some alley
weirdly lit by a couch on fire, that I
drag my extinction in search of you....

Past the guarded schoolyards, the boarded-up churches, swastikaed
synagogues, defended houses of worship, past
newspapered windows of tenements, among the violated,
the prosecuted citizenry, throughout this
storied, buttressed, scavenged, policed
city I call home, in which I am a guest....

A bruise, blue
in the muscle, you
impinge upon me.
As bone hugs the ache home, so
I'm vexed to love you, your body

the shape of returns, your hair a torso
of light, your heat
I must have, your opening

I'd eat, each moment
of that soft-finned fruit,
inverted fountain in which I don't see me.

My tongue remembers your wounded flavor.
The vein in my neck
adores you. A sword
stands up between my hips,
my hidden fleece sends forth its scent of human oil.

The shadows under my arms,
I promise, are tender, the shadows
under my face. Do not calculate,
but come, smooth other, rough sister.
Yet, how will you know me

among the captives, my hair grown long,
my blood motley, my ways trespassed upon?
In the uproar, the confusion
of accents and inflections,
how will you hear me when I open my mouth?

Look for me, one of the drab population
under fissured edifices, fractured
artifices. Make my various
names flock overhead,
I will follow you.
Hew me to your beauty.

Stack in me the unaccountable fire,
bring on me the iron leaf, but tenderly.
Folded one hundred times and
creased, I'll not crack.
Threshed to excellence, I'll achieve you.

But in the city
in which I love you,
no one comes, no one

meets me in the brick clefts;
in the wedged dark,

no finger touches me secretly, no mouth
tastes my flawless salt,
no one wakens the honey in the cells, finds the humming
in the ribs, the rich business in the recesses;
hulls clogged, I continue laden, translated

by exhaustion and time's appetite, my sleep abandoned
in bus stations and storefront stoops,
my insomnia erected under a sky
cross-hatched by wires, branches,
and black flights of rain. Lewd body of wind

jams me in the passageways, doors slam
like guns going off, a gun goes off, a pie plate spins
past, whizzing its thin tremolo,
a plastic bag, fat with wind, barrels by and slaps
a chain-link fence, wraps it like clung skin.

In the excavated places,
I waited for you, and I did not cry out.
In the derelict rooms, my body needed you,
and there was such flight in my breast.
During the daily assaults, I called to you,

and my voice pursued you,
even backward
to that other city
in which I saw a woman
squat in the street

beside a body,
and fan with a handkerchief flies from its face.
That woman
was not me. And
the corpse

lying there, lying there
so still it seemed with great effort, as though
his whole being was concentrating on the hole
in his forehead, so still
I expected he'd sit up any minute and laugh out loud:

that man was not me;
his wound was his, his death not mine.
And the soldier
who fired the shot, then lit a cigarette:
he was not me.

And the ones I do not see
in cities all over the world,
the ones sitting, standing, lying down, those
in prisons playing checkers with their knocked-out teeth:
they are not me. Some of them are

my age, even my height and weight;
none of them is me.
The woman who is slapped, the man who is kicked,
the ones who don't survive,
whose names I do not know;

they are not me forever,
the ones who no longer live
in the cities in which
you are not,
the cities in which I looked for you.

The rain stops, the moon
in her breaths appears overhead.
The only sound now is a far flapping.
Over the National Bank, the flag of some republic or other
gallops like water or fire to tear itself away.

If I feel the night
move to disclosures or crescendos,

it's only because I'm famished
for meaning; the night
merely dissolves.

And your otherness is perfect as my death.
Your otherness exhausts me,
like looking suddenly up from here
to impossible stars fading.
Everything is punished by your absence.

Is prayer, then, the proper attitude
for the mind that longs to be freely blown,
but which gets snagged on the barb
called *world*, that
tooth-ache, the actual? What prayer

would I build? And to whom?
Where are you
in the cities in which I love you,
the cities daily risen to work and to money,
to the magnificent miles and the gold coasts?

Morning comes to this city vacant of you.
Pages and windows flare, and you are not there.
Someone sweeps his portion of sidewalk,
wakens the drunk, slumped like laundry,
and you are gone.

You are not in the wind
which someone notes in the margins of a book.
You are gone out of the small fires in abandoned lots
where human figures huddle,
each aspiring to its own ghost.

Between brick walls, in a space no wider than my face,
a leafless sapling stands in mud.
In its branches, a nest of raw mouths
gaping and cheeping, scrawny fires that must eat.

My hunger for you is no less than theirs.
At the gates of the city in which I love you,
the sea hauls the sun on its back,
strikes the land, which rebukes it.
What ardor in its sliding heft,
a flameless friction on the rocks.

Like the sea, I am recommended by my orphaning.
Noisy with telegrams not received,
quarrelsome with aliases,
intricate with misguided journeys,
by my expulsions have I come to love you.

Straight from my father's wrath,
and long from my mother's womb,
late in this century and on a Wednesday morning,
bearing the mark of one who's experienced
neither heaven nor hell,

my birthplace vanished, my citizenship earned,
in league with stones of the earth, I
enter, without retreat or help from history,
the days of no day, my earth
of no earth, I re-enter

the city in which I love you.
And I never believed that the multitude
of dreams and many words were vain.

OCEAN VUONG

NOTEBOOK FRAGMENTS

A scar's width of warmth on a worn man's neck.
>That's all I wanted to be.

Sometimes I ask for too much just to feel my mouth overflow.

Discovery: My longest pubic hair is 1.2 inches.

Good or bad?

7:18 a.m. Kevin overdosed last night. His sister left a message.
>Couldn't listen to all of it. That makes three this year.

I promise to stop soon.

Spilled orange juice all over the table this morning. Sudden
>sunlight I couldn't wipe away.

All through the night my hands were daylight.

Woke at 1 a.m and, for no reason, ran through Duffy's cornfield.
>Boxers only.

Corn was dry. I sounded like a fire, for no reason.

Grandma said *In the war they would grab a baby, a soldier at each*
>*ankle, and pull . . . Just like that.*

It's finally spring! Daffodils everywhere.
>Just like that.

There are over 13,000 unidentified body parts from the World
Trade Center being stored in an underground repository in New
York City.

Good or bad?

Shouldn't heaven be superheavy by now?
Maybe the rain is 'sweet' because it falls
          through so much of the world.

Even sweetness can scratch the throat, so stir the sugar well. —Grandma

4:37 a.m. How come depression makes me feel more alive?

Life is funny.

Note to self: If a guy tells you his favorite poet is Jack Kerouac,
          there's a very good chance he's a douchebag.

Note to self: If Orpheus were a woman I wouldn't be stuck
          down here.

Why do all my books leave me empty-handed?

In Vietnamese, the word for grenade is 'bom', from the French
          'pomme', meaning 'apple'.

Or was it American for 'bomb'?

Woke up screaming with no sound. The room filling with a
bluish water called dawn. Went to kiss grandma on the forehead

just in case.

An American soldier fucked a Vietnamese farmgirl. Thus my
mother exists. Thus I exist. Thus no bombs = no family = no me.

Yikes.

9:47 a.m. Jerked off four times already. My arm kills.
Eggplant = cà pháo = 'grenade tomato'. Thus nourishment
          defined by extinction.

I met a man tonight. A high school English teacher
        from the next town. A small town. Maybe

I shouldn't have, but he had the hands
        of someone I used to know. Someone I was used to.

The way they formed brief churches
        over the table as he searched for the right words.

I met a man, not you. In his room the Bibles shook on the shelf
        from candlelight. His scrotum a bruised fruit. I kissed it

lightly, the way one might kiss a grenade
        before hurling it into the night's mouth.

Maybe the tongue is also a key.

Yikes.

I could eat you he said, brushing my cheek with his knuckles.

I think I love my mom very much.

Some grenades explode with a vision of white flowers.

Baby's breath blooming in a darkened sky, across
        my chest.

Maybe the tongue is also a pin.

I'm gonna lose it when Whitney Houston dies.

I met a man. I promise to stop.

A pillaged village is a fine example of perfect rhyme. He said that.

He was white. Or maybe, I was just beside myself, next to him.

Either way, I forgot his name by heart.

I wonder what it feels like to move at the speed of thirst—if it's
    fast as lying on the kitchen floor with the lights off.

(Kristopher)

6:24 a.m. Greyhound station. One-way ticket to New York
    City: $36.75.

6:57 a.m. I love you, mom.

When the prison guards burned his manuscripts, Nguyễn
    Chí Thiện couldn't stop laughing—the 238 poems
    already inside him.

I dreamed I walked barefoot all the way to your house in the
    snow. Everything was the blue of smudged ink

and you were still alive. There was even a light the shade of
    sunrise inside your window.

God must be a season, grandma said, looking out at the blizzard
    drowning her garden.

My footsteps on the sidewalk were the smallest flights.

Dear god, if you *are* a season, let it be the one I passed through
    to get here.

Here. That's all I wanted to be.

I promise.

KAREN RIGBY

THE STORY OF ADAM AND EVE

Boucicaut Master and Workshop, c. 1415

illuminare

Their spines must have aged
like hooks, those brothers painting
in cold rooms: deep blue
and olive snaking
down a tree. They must have beaten
gold-leaf for each thumbnail,
God pressed in goatskin
every hour. What do I know
about illuminating books, the bowl of saffron
turned to stone? Who remembers
kingfishers on water?

*

Before the serpent. Before the beasts
lay on their paws, before stones released their heat.
Before the savage machinery.
A woman sprung from bone facing her husband,
his body inside her, his body a wing
in thickened amber—

*

—as in the riffling surface
        of things revealed. As in the palm turned
                to the word flensed
                        from the body of God,

        as in the first breath murmured in the man's lungs

          and how I understood
when the city blacked out

          and substations powered off,
                              sudden downpour
at midday, women in voile skirts
          clinging like seaweed—

                    *

          In fifteenth century Paris
     the manuscript inked with quills
                    cut from a swan
               becomes a measure
     of the will, but also of the vine.

               *

About the beginning
I could tell you the garden bloomed
multiple bells. I could say
everything I know about beauty I learned
from the body's ruin:
the rib drawn
through his quartered skin,
the skin sewn and the woman born,
a dark homunculus.
          I could listen
     for the first rasp like the hinge
on a storm door and I would know
the beginning was the word, but also the soot.
Also the lie.

               *

Think of the parchmenter scraping

his curved blade

cutting double-leaves   soaked in lime

Think of the calligrapher

gesso   lamp-black   oak gall   mineral pigments

the book revealing what *bereft* means:

field whelmed with salt

crows echoing their brothers the songbirds

city of exiles given to powdered iron.

EUGENIA LEIGH

SELAH

When the sky unhinges, how will we survive?

Who will extract the cancers
from our lips, the bombs from our arteries?

When we make delirious love
in the closets of our small, lovestarved God,
may he honor

our passion. Forgive
our poisons. May he unplug our churches—
fling every cracked bulb

back into the sky. And with each re-tinseled constellation, may he
        grow.
Like a hot organ. May he watch us come, come to understand

worship. That to worship is to survive is to be

wholly human, wholly
gripping the other hand.

MIA AYUMI MALHOTRA

THE LOSING BEGINS

for Isako, at last

Long before you're gone, the losing begins.
And slow. And slow. You let go in inches,
starting with the shoulders, the ulna, wrist,
until each hand is rung with light. I never
imagined it this way. How the body goes
in stages. And the mind, leeched through
a crack at the base of the skull. No name
for this, though it's the word that makes it
bearable. The edge, blunted. Run, I will
run from this. The world caws brightly,
the crown of my head bursts with youth.
Yet this is how it ends. Who will bear this
dark shard in the eye, that the end when
it comes, dresses us down without mercy?
Small wonder, the racket you made at
the child's approach. Ha—ha! To skeletal
teeth in head, bared. To flat hands, palms
clapped bone against bone, *thwack thwack*,
warding off demons as they gather like grim
congregants around your bed. This strange
anointing. This new spirit. How we fend.

LI-YOUNG LEE

ARISE, GO DOWN

It wasn't the bright hems of the Lord's skirts
that brushed my face and I opened my eyes
to see from a cleft in rock His backside;

it's a wasp perched on my left cheek. I keep
my eyes closed and stand perfectly still
in the garden till it leaves me alone,

not to contemplate how this century
ends and the next begins with no one
I know having seen God, but to wonder

why I get through most days unscathed, though I
live in a time when it might be otherwise,
and I grow more fatherless each day.

For years now I have come to conclusions
without my father's help, discovering
on my own what I know, what I don't know,

and seeing how one cancels the other.
I've become a scholar of cancellations.
Here, I stand among my father's roses

and see that what punctures outnumbers what
consoles, the cruel and the tender never
make peace, though one climbs, though one descends

petal by petal to the hidden ground
no one owns. I see that which is taken
away by violence or persuasion.

The rose announces on earth the kingdom
of gravity. A bird cancels it.

My eyelids cancel the bird. Anything

might cancel my eyes: distance, time, war.
My father said, *Never take your both eyes*
off of the world, before he rocked me.

All night we waited for the knock
that would have signalled, All clear, come now;
it would have meant escape; it never came.

I didn't make the world I leave you with,
he said, and then, being poor, he left me
only this world, in which there is always

a family waiting in terror
before they're rended, this world wherein a man
might arise, go down, and walk along a path

and pause and bow to roses, roses
his father raised, and admire them, for one moment
unable, thank God, to see in each and
every flower the world cancelling itself.

NEIL AITKEN

HOW WE ARE SAVED

Gathered at the side of my father's bed, his body still
warm to the touch, his eyes darkening like those of a fish
laid high on the river bank, the sun slipping through
the half-closed blinds into the cream-colored room—
we have come to dress him one last time.

To bend his arms, not for prayer, but to slide the sleeves
of the clean white shirt over, to pull each limb through—
pants, socks, shoes—till the body is clothed, readied at last
to meet whatever fiery light will embrace it first. The kiln,
the grave, love's small white cloud that arrives just before rain.

No, this is just a body. Clay and water. Hollow. What we shed
in the white room over words of prayer. What we weave of memory,
grace for grace, this already faded circle of thought and longing.
Oh, this body—grown more wind than flesh, even as the air leaves
his lungs not to return, there is a knocking at the door, something dark
and hopeful rising to my lips, the strains of a very old song.

BRYNN SAITO

REINCARNATION

Imagine your bird-self—white thorn and cinquefoil
winding their way up the August mountain.

Slow-moving creatures with full bones and focus
lunge through the understory—

What do they know about flower-walking, flight moons—
their clicks and their fascia, their hesitant

assembly? In the garden, in childhood: you lead:
one sister pulling the other through laughter palms,

jasmine. Then two turn to ash, scattered by sons
over phantom orchids. Now the lake dawns

with blue defeat—a bottled invitation. You sing again
your fear-song, certain she's somewhere in the morning light.

TINA CHANG

THE BURNING

> "...I've lived without names..."
> **—Stephen Kuusisto**

Off a seashore in Russia I run, laughing
at the mystery of movement in the form
of water, laughing at my father with sand
on his face who will one day die.

Or imagine for a minute a locomotive
full of people, rocking with the motion
of a vintage sorrow, head bowing as if
time has beaten them. In my winter season

I think of monks in Penang who sit without
sound for weeks. How they live inside silence.
The silence is alive. The ringing of a bell
is an intricate acorn; my soul hits the ground

when it falls. The apple for all its perfection
will never change. The seed I swallow fashions
a knot in my throat, the fiber of the peel winds
like a staircase leading me down. I look

at my teeth-marks in fruit, in flesh
like a message, an erotic code deciphered
by tearing and biting down. I want to keep
this braille, this transcript of my soul:

My body is a vessel of wanting.
My body is a vessel of fury.
My body is a vessel of apology.

I am the thread & the damage the thread made after the mending.
I am the god I don't know & the fire that burns with no fuel.

SOFIA M. STARNES

NIGHTLIFE

The moon dissolves to mist
and flower; the window balances the outside dark

against a single lamp—
and underneath, a rose. Some nights, I know

three things: *the being rush,*
bone sequence, hide and blood, bliss of these rudiments,

from them to make a life.
                         And then, some slower

things: *the being wait,* a portal, mouthful, ache;
the knob that clicks comes loose; the hinge that stalls

holds hard.   Pause, pause—
The evening brings the undisguise of things:

the bowtie stars, the myrtle crook still blooming
beside the drive;

the moonlight satisfies the alcove glow of what I know.
                        The being pluck,

the toughest being of all, out of the garden lush,
ten thousand reds, ten thousand fickle golds, toadstools

on grass. At last, the unequal rose
climbs on the bow-blade clip, a summer-seize.

           I do not fear the many from which I come.
           I do not fear the many to which I go.

Some nights, a single look for everything I lose,

a single hope

by which I'll candle back.
A nipple dribs its moon, the moonbeam dries, lipborne

into a child.
Between the moon and rose, the hourglass.

JANE WONG

AFTER PREPARING THE ALTAR, THE GHOSTS FEAST FEVERISHLY

> "How hard it is to sleep
> in the middle of a life"
> **–Audre Lorde**

We wake in the middle of a life,   hungry.
We smear durian   along our mouths, sing soft
death a lullaby. Carcass breath, eros of licked fingers
and the finest perfume. What is love if not   rot?
We wear the fruit's hull as a spiked crown, grinning
in green armor.   Death to the grub, fat in his milky
shuffle! Death to the lawlessness   of dirt! Death
to mud and its false chocolate!   To the bloated sun
we want to slice open and yolk   all over
the village. We want a sun-drenched   slug feast,
an omelet loosening its folds like hot Jell-O. We want
the marbled fat of steak and all   its swirling pink
galaxies. We want the drool, the gnash, the pluck of
each corn kernel, raw and summer   swell.
Tears welling up   oil. Order up! Pickled
cucumbers piled like logs for a fire, like fat limbs we
pepper and succulent   in.   Order up: shrimp
chips curling in a porcelain bowl like subway seats.
Grapes peeled from bitter bark – almost translucent,
like eyes we would rather see.   Little girl, what do you
leave, leaven   in your sight? Death to the open
eyes of the dying. Here,   there are so many open
eyes we can't close each one.   No, we did not say

the steamed eye of a fish. No eyelids fluttering like
no butterfly wings. No purple yam lips. We said eyes.
Still and resolute as a heartbreaker.   Does this break
your heart?   Look, we don't want
to be rude, but seconds, please. Want: globes of oranges
swallowed whole like a basketball or Mars or whatever
planet is the most delicious.   Slather Saturn!
Ferment Mercury!   Lap up its film of dust!
Seconds, thirds, fourths! Meat wool! A bouquet of
chicken feet! A garden of   melons, monstrous
in their bulge!   Prune back nothing. We purr
in this garden. We comb through berries and come out
so blue. Little girl,   lasso tofu, the rope
slicing its belly clean. Deep fry a cloud so it tastes like
bitter gourd or your father leaving – the exhaust of
his car, charred. Serenade a snake and slither its tongue
into yours and   bite. Love! What is love
if not knotted in garlic? Child, we move through graves
like eels, delicious   with our heads first, our mouths
agape. Our teeth: little needles to stitch a factory of
everything made in China.   You ask: are you hungry?
Hunger eats through the air like ozone. You ask: what
does it mean to be rootless? Roots are good to use as
toothpicks. You: how can you wake in the middle of
a life? We shut and open our eyes like the sun shining
on tossed pennies in a forgotten well. Bald copper,
blood. Yu choy bolts   into roses down here.
While you were sleeping, we woke to the old leaves
of your backyard shed and ate that and one of your
lost flip flops too. In a future life, we saw rats overtake
a supermarket with so much milk, we turned opaque.

Jane Wong

We wake to something boiling. We wake to wash dirt
from lettuce, to blossom into your face. Aphids along
the lashes. Little girl, don't forget   to take care
of the chickens, squawking in their mess and stench.
Did our mouths buckle   at the sight
of you devouring slice   after slice of pizza and
the greasy box too? Does this frontier swoon for you?
It's time to wake up. Wake the tapeworm who loves
his home. Wake the ants,   let them do-si-do
a spoonful of peanut butter. Tell us, little girl, are you
hungry, awake,   astonished enough?

E. J. KOH

SHAMAN

If you want to take
up space, first see

how small you are
like rocks, honey-

combs, and charcoal
anchoring, feeding,

heating. In the sky
the clouds are combed

like rabbit fur. If I
remember this, I am

not dreaming. You place
the flowered twig

behind my ear, mark
of my learning you

in bluebell, a person
small like me, but higher.

TIMOTHY LIU

TRANSCENDENCE

One can live without language.
Without a decent paying job.

Just ask those Moroccan boys

with towels wrapped around their
waists as they lead you into

the rearmost chamber so full

of eucalyptus steam your eyes
take several minutes to grow

accustomed to that hot dark—

a piece of black soap dropped
into your lap as you rub the thing

over every square inch except

your face, everyone here sinking
their feet into a bucket of water

at a local hammam known for

modesty, leaving nothing
but a pair of shorts on, nakedness

an affront, the layers of our selves

scrubbed off, nothing left behind
but little grey worms sloughed off

by a rough mitt as you lay there

Timothy Liu

unplugged, smart phone going dead
in a country where your adaptor

prongs no longer fit the holes—

MATTHEW OLZMANN

LETTER TO A BRIDGE MADE OF ROPE—

I don't trust you. To the shepherd, herding his flock
through the gorge below, it must appear as if I walk
on the sky. I feel like that too: so little between me

and The Fall. But this is how faith works its craft.
One foot set in front of the other, while the wind
rattles the cage of the living, and the rocks down there

cheer every wobble, and your threads keep
this braided business almost intact saying: *Don't worry.*
I've been here a long time. You'll make it across.

KAREN RIGBY

CEBOLLA CHURCH

Georgia O'Keeffe, 1945

The desert is a lion-colored seam.

Not a finger of dust lines sills—
not a spine or lizard scale.

It could be any thumb-shaped blur
against the window pane:

sexton. Thief.

Before villagers bring stems
sliced beneath cold faucets,

someone has to sweep.
Someone lights the long, pitched room

like the hold of a ship,
stacks books beneath each bench.

Because the face held
by the hand recedes,

it could be the soul itself
gazing out of the Santo Niño church,

beyond clay erasures.

One month, news kept looping
the same reel of the last wreck.

Men roamed like beekeepers
in their white suits.

Karen Rigby

I pictured walls radiating gold—
the church with its slant door.

Someone listening
for a distant thundering.

E. J. KOH

FLOATERS

He pointed to himself and then to a patch of weeds
to show the difference between Man & Plant.
He gestured at the space between his index & thumb,
and said, *there has to be a middle point, which would be Animal.*

In order—the root & the fox & the infant.
He looked at me then and said,
I will not live to know
if there's a room between Man & God.

Then the sound of his oil lamp swinging and the wildflowers
(that die & grow over their own clusters) move closer
to his log steps—which he could not climb now
without the aid of a cane.

He asked me what floaters looked like, something he thought
his old mind could not notice. Once we were outside,
he said, *Ask me what the shapes of angels looked like then.*
He recognized the clouds he had seen as a boy.

BRYAN THAO WORRA

ONI

My demons have names I try to keep
    To myself
A scimitar smile as I walk with them in Spring
A snarl and a python handshake

     That wants to slither away with you

II.

Am I a dog in Demon State
Or a demon in Dog City?

Easy to say, difficult to believe,
I can show you the way, in either case

III.

I miss the cherry blossoms of DC
My little memories rattling like the Metro
      Through Farragut Station

IV.

Rest, Mishima,
Rest your beautiful skull
In the field by Ono no Komachi.

Dream amid the leaves and stone walls,
Let the wind shout of forgotten Yamato for you.

It's been 30 years already.
You're becoming a cartoon
While the girl is an idle monk's mocking brush stroke.

V.

Could Sojobo have slain Shuten Doji?
Unworthy speculation!

Your pen should be remembering the slaughter
       Of Khoua Her's tiny waifs,
       Or the death of Tong Kue,
       The drowned of the Mekong,
Or even poor Vincent Chin
Struggling for his last breath
Beneath Detroit bats
Devoid of pity

VI.

No matter what I shout,
There isn't a stone on the earth that will shatter today.

SHANKAR NARAYAN

THREE-SPIRIT PRAYER BEFORE THE TANDAV

Because Lord, no journey knows who I really am. Because I feel silicon
draining chances to find you in this life. Because it is you who commutes

these lines of freeway, three lines of ash on your forehead
all that's left after the end of the last universe. Because the shlokas appear everywhere now—

bullets for grey wolves in Cascadia, missing green geckos in Delhi, iceless Arctic
walruses, white bears leaping from desperate

outcrops onto the bloodied backs of belugas. Because these things unhome me. Because you wandered
the villages with only a stray for company, and because this life of yours

is against time. Because how many times
has your maya sucked me in, in

how many cedar-bodies have I inverted my essence, capillaries and spleen and aorta and femurs and skull
and DNA sequences, because how I have tried to reduce myself to dispassionate bytes

only to be dragged back by your lovemaking, your lightning-tongues
on my nipples and your fangs encircling the apple of my poison-

throat. Because I mire in threes—my body, another body, and the galaxy
of you, who cries when I come, who sedates me to sanctuary out of clutch

of the so many ways we die before death. So Lord, lotus to my dust-

feet, be merciful—let my lovers touch my real body. Just once, let them come nameless
like dogwood petals. And only then permit the apocalypse.

ED BOK LEE

RANDOM FLOATING CELLS WITH STYLE

To love one another with quantum certainty is to volumize the stars.

It might take some time, a few million years, but for your efforts—
   many more

moth-white, fuzzy, brightened blurs. There, someone

once upon a time loved despite. There, another

just shed enough fears in love not to burst. Each evening,

this movie of love plays out like popcorn blinking lively in the sky.

As if your epilogue were an ancient, omniscient satellite to whom

time no longer matters, and matter always exceeds the count.

Ah, you bonus illumination in this vast multiplying apart.

You gathering of random floating cells with style.

You—all of you—dying trillions of times every hour

to recommence each new forever inside these eyes. Look.

Look at me seeing you seeing me from the beginning of the
   universe and time.

Never forget: wherever, whenever you are, is the history of all you
   love in the dark.

FAISAL MOHYUDDIN

GHAZAL FOR THE LOST

None of the unspeaking souls on this morning train knows where
    we are going.
Waking again to a washed-clean darkness, we prefer the
    frightening disquiet of mystery.

To bear witness to the disappearing bravery of the night's last
    remaining star
Is to walk alone through the hills without water, is to fill your
    mouth with mystery.

Inside each bird in the taxidermist's house, hidden between folds
    of crumpled paper—
The photograph of a child, bright eyes of a surrogate heart, their
    youthful mystery.

Why must every breath come at a cost? Each passing minute
    steal from us the color
And strength of our bodies? To live is to be a dying thing, all else
    is mystery.

Prayer directs our longing toward Mecca, keeps our foreheads
    anchored to the earth.
Each step is touched by language, but between prostrations:
    silence, and mystery.

When the rain begins to fall, sending shivers of joy through the
    dead desert air,
A sleeping dog lifts his head from the sand, watches the washing
    away of mystery.

As you arrive at your final destination, a village carved from a
    mountain's hip,
A castle at its center, drop your body, begin to climb, be no
    longer afraid of mystery.

Do you remember, Faisal, what the elders preached about
    forgetting? Centuries of grief
Had made them wise, taught them to seek the mercy and
    goodness of mystery.

LESLIEANN HOBAYAN

DEAR HOME,

Capiz shell windows. Jeepneys. The sea.

White house, red shutters. Sunburst Lane bursting with sun. Dirt bikes and skinned knees, the white boy who held my hand, loved me at nine.

Pancit and lumpia. Lechon and kare-kare. Baptisms, communions, first place math team. Basketball in driveways and A Tribe Called Quest. Line dancing and cotillions. Tinikling and karaoke.

Have you been swept out to sea by Typhoon Haiyan, brushed away with Samar, Lolo's hometown, like crumbs off a table, the rugged sound of Visaya buried in water?

Or dissolved into the memories of elders who have forgotten how to speak?

Have you run away from this girl bursting with sun? Does the touch of my hand singe?

Perhaps you are my children's laughter sprinkled over tea parties. A full spread of plastic cakes and My Little Ponies. Tiny cups of hot chocolate. The snow outside whipping against the window.

Maybe you are the sound of a church choir singing "Be Not Afraid", voices echoing in the rafters. The Body of Christ melting on my tongue.

Perhaps you are the taste of Om in my mouth. Though Sherlin is not a lane of sunburst, the shine still slides along driveways staccatoed by basketballs and rim shots. The smell of damp leaves and charred husks of grilled corn. Adobo slowly cooking on the stove.

But maybe not.

Perhaps you have been right here all along, deep in my belly: a fire.

VIJAY SESHADRI

THE LONG MEADOW

Near the end of one of the old poems, the son of righteousness,
the source of virtue and civility,
on whose back the kingdom is carried
as on the back of the tortoise the earth is carried,
passes into the next world.
The wood is dark. The wood is dark,
and on the other side of the wood the sea is shallow, warm, endless.
In and around it, there is no threat of life—
so little is the atmosphere charged with possibility that
he might as well be wading through a flooded basement.
He wades for what seems like forever,
and never stops to rest in the shade of the metal raintrees
springing out of the water at fixed intervals.
Time, though endless, is also short,
so he wades on, until he walks out of the sea and into the mountains,
where he burns on the windward slopes and freezes in the valleys.
After unendurable struggles,
he finally arrives at the celestial realm.
The god waits there for him. The god invites him to enter.
But looking through the glowing portal,
he sees on that happy plain not those he thinks wait eagerly for him—

42

his beloved, his brothers, his companions in war and exile,
all long since dead and gone—
but, sitting pretty and enjoying the gorgeous sunset,
his cousin and bitter enemy, the cause of that war, that exile,
whose arrogance and vicious indolence
plunged the world into grief.
The god informs him that, yes, those he loved have been carried down
the river of fire. Their thirst for justice
offended the cosmic powers, who are jealous of justice.
In their place in the celestial realm, called Alaukika in the ancient texts,
the breaker of faith is now glorified.
He, at least, acted in keeping with his nature.
Who has not felt a little of the despair the son of righteousness now feels,
staring wildly around him?
The god watches, not without compassion and a certain wonder.
This is the final illusion,
the one to which all the others lead.
He has to pierce through it himself, without divine assistance.
He will take a long time about it,
with only his dog to keep him company,
the mongrel dog, celebrated down the millennia,

who has waded with him,
shivered and burned with him,
and never abandoned him to his loneliness.
That dog bears a slight resemblance to my dog,
a skinny, restless, needy, overprotective mutt,
who was rescued from a crack house by Suzanne.
On weekends, and when I can shake free during the week,
I take her to the Long Meadow, in Prospect Park, where dogs
are allowed off the leash in the early morning.
She's gray-muzzled and old now, but you can't tell that by the way she runs.

WANTING TO GET CLEAR ON HER GOD-THINKING,
SHE WENT OUT INTO THAT MEADOW AGAIN:
LOCATING THE DIVINE IN THE NATURAL WORLD

BRYNN SAITO

HOW TO PREPARE THE MIND FOR LIGHTNING

In the recesses of the woman's mind
      there is a warehouse. The warehouse
           is covered in wisteria. The wisteria wonders

what it is doing in the mind of the woman.
      The woman wonders too.
           The river is raw tonight. The river is a calling

aching with want. The woman walks towards it
      her arms unimpaired and coated
           with moonlight. The wisteria wants the river.

It also wants the warehouse in the mind
      of the woman, wants to remain in the ruins
           though water is another kind of original ruin

determined in its structure and unpredictable.
      The woman unlaces the light across her body.
           She wades through the river while twining wisteria

bleeds from her mouth, her eyes, her wrist-veins,
      her heart valve, her heart. The garden again
           overgrows the body—called by the water

and carried by the woman to the wanting river.
      When she bleeds the wisteria, the warehouse
           in her mind is free and empty and the source

of all emptiness. It is free to house the night sky.
      It is free like the woman to hold nothing
           but the boundless, empty, unimaginable dark.

JENNIFER S. CHENG

FROM DEAR BLANK SPACE

Dear Invisible House

What we are building. A ghost or something to recall the void.
When I was a child, I read that God was a shadow hovering
above the waters. Instead, one might say "Sacred" or "Truth"
or "Language." Either way we could sense something in the
distance, in the fog, and because we are human, we reached out
to see if we could touch it.

*

Dear Wilderness

Alone in the forest, stranded at sea, wandering in the desert—the
kinds of stories that move me are the ones where we continue to
find ourselves shrouded in the unknowingness of being. Every
day begins and ends like this: the galaxies are ever moving away
from you. Inside the planetarium, I leaned into the swathy
darkness, and somewhere scientists sensed an unknown, invisible
web holding the universe together, to which they gave the name
"dark matter" and "dark energy." Projected on the ceiling, it
looks like a vast and intricate skein parachuting our bodies. In
my favorite essay by Fanny Howe, she starts, "Bewilderment as
a poetics and an ethics," and from the body of text that follows,
a vocabulary emerges like a collection of nodes: *mystery, hidden,
unlocatable, complexities, perplexities, errancy, fluidity, spiraling.*

*

Dear Void

And what is a constellation anyway, but a shape we temporarily trace in that vast pause, a lyric of geometry we speak into an otherwise dark and uncertain space?

*

Dear Rest Note

By which I mean, if it is not yet clear, *form as language*. I mean: The shadowy white of the page. Measures of emptiness, an absence of sounds, as part of the vocabulary. Writers say *form* and *language,* as if they are distinct elements of consideration, but I am interested in tensions of space, pockets of text amidst silent tracts, as a kind of language in itself. It is true that we speak different languages, we learn different native tongues, and sometimes, in an unexpected arrangement of stars and space, we find a discourse for what we could never before say.

*

Dear Open Mouths

The silent ones, the broken ones, the ones who are lost. If there is a peculiar but intuitive relationship between the inarticulable and the sacred, there is also a relationship between the sacred and what is broken. Think: Body. In the Sermon on the Mount of my childhood, it is the meek who inherit the earth. It is the weak who are strong. If I take this logic further: the voiceless who are most articulate.

*

Dear Archive of Ghosts

You are traces of a mollusk after it has slithered away. You are traffic moving outside my window, softened into a melody I can bear. You are breaking morning and falling evening, when the house is most flooded with shadows and angles. You are inhale, then exhale, my intentions and my failures. You are condensations of the air between us. You are interstices, the heart conditions of an immigrant perpetually arriving and departing, or how we are all itinerants; a map of evaporations. If the world is a thing that cannot be spoken whole, then let me stay a little bit broken, a relief to acknowledge this pile of occluded things.

*

Dear Decreation

We were taught that God is a hard slate, like stone, but I found it deafening as water. In 1933 Junichiro Tanizaki wrote in an essay, *In Praise of Shadows*, "I would have the eaves deep and the walls dark, I would push back into the shadows the things that come forward too clearly." Decades later, having intuited through mathematics what they cannot know, scientists hypothesize what they cannot see: an unknown variable beyond the observable galaxy, a "shadow universe" whose shape we infer indirectly, poring through and in between space like a tenuous, veiny map: undefinable, yet literally keeping it all together. "It is by following the light that we have been led into the dark."

*

Dear Decreation II

Sometimes it is the ruined structure that I am building— splintered, turmoiled, mystified. To catch the bare bones of it, the slivers of darkness and hunger in between. To remind me that ruin is where we started, and every construction is a false veneer, a red herring. Sometimes, the closest sense of wholeness comes from holding the pieces loosely. Perhaps the failure, and beauty, of language, the world, is this: that meaning is found in its recesses.

*

Dear Longing

A poetics of blank space, then: "The visible world is soon
emblematic of the intentions of the invisible." Some days I
wake and the fog is already crowding my window, my little
green plants, and I know what humans have known since the
beginning: we belong and also we do not belong. Somehow
we sensed how the fabric surrounding us was not whole but
punctured through. Our bodies absorbed a tempo: we search,
we suffer, and we search again. In the midst of a buried hour
when everything around me is sleeping and straining and I do
not know how shallow or deep, my friend H writes to me from
the other side of the world: "Prayer cannot exist if there's any
certainty that it will be heard." This, I suspect, is at the heart of
the contradiction that propels me, though I barely know what it
means.

*

Dear Series of Intersecting Circles, Moon Cycles

In the end, we recognized something in such a cadence of
eclipses and absences, of constant bewildering loss. Instead
of oppressive concreteness: a brokenness to teach us longing.
Instead, a collection of language shifting and tumbling in the
dark: *void, holes, broken, fractured, liminal, limbo, murky, obscured,
shadows, night, wilderness, wandering, lost, uncertainty, ambiguity,
speculation, hidden, unrepresented, unrepresentable, inarticulable,
unknowable, unreachable,*

*

Dear [   ]

So I hold you, and I lose you. We are always all a little bit drowning. To investigate the world in the rhythms of a swimmer: to go for deep dives and come up for air; to hold my body half-under.

LI-YOUNG LEE

HAVE YOU PRAYED?

When the wind
turns and asks, in my father's voice,
Have you prayed?

I know three things. One:
I'm never finished answering to the dead.

Two: A man is four winds and three fires.
And the four winds are his father's voice,
his mother's voice . . .

Or maybe he's seven winds and ten fires.
And the fires are seeing, hearing, touching,
dreaming, thinking . . .
Or is he the breath of God?

When the wind turns traveler
and asks, in my father's voice, *Have you prayed?*
I remember three things.
One: A father's love

is milk and sugar,
two-thirds worry, two-thirds grief, and what's left over

is trimmed and leavened to make the bread
the dead and the living share.

And patience? That's to endure
the terrible leavening and kneading.

And wisdom? That's my father's face in sleep.

When the wind
asks, *Have you prayed?*

I know it's only me

reminding myself
a flower is one station between
earth's wish and earth's rapture, and blood

was fire, salt, and breath long before
it quickened any wand or branch, any limb
that woke speaking. It's just me

in the gowns of the wind,
or my father through me, asking,
Have you found your refuge yet?
asking, *Are you happy?*

Strange. A troubled father. A happy son.
The wind with a voice. And me talking to no one.

BARBARA JANE REYES

[GALLEON PRAYER]

pilipinas to petatlán

she whispers desert trees, thorn-ridged, trickling yellow candles;
roots spilling snakes' blood
virgin of ribboned silk; virgin of gold filigree
one day's walk westward, a crucifix of fisherman's dinghy
dimensions washes ashore
virgin adorned in robe of shark embryo and coconut husk
she fingers mollusks, wraps herself in sea vines
virgin of ocean voyage peril
she wills herself born
virgin of mud brick ruins; virgin of sandstorm echoes
she is saint of commonplaces; saint of badlands
virgin of jade, camphor, porcelain; virgin of barter for ghosts
penitents, earthdivers of forgotten names praying skyward
virgin of scars blossomed from open veins of fire
she slips across the pacific's rivers of pearldiving children
virgin of copper coins
she is bloodletting words, painting unlikeness
virgin of anachronism
children stained with berries and rust, their skeletons bend,
arrow-tipped; smoke blurs eyes' edges
virgin of mineral depletion; virgin of mercury
at other altitudes she remembers to breathe; a monument
scraping cloud
virgin of tin deposits extracted from mountains
these are not divinations; there is goldleaf about her skin
virgin of naming and renaming places in between

E. J. KOH

THE MOUNTAIN

She protects silence. She communes with it by sitting.
She holds onto it by giving up endlessly.

She gets bigger, smaller. She feels burdened by effort
—by distance crossed by the dark.

She takes comfort in doing nothing.
She loses her own importance. She believes in defenselessness,

then lightness. Deep in her heart, she waits for the end.
She tows in time; earns her breaking.

No one knows why she weeps as bright as memory.
When asked, she says, *The end must come first.*

W. TODD KANEKO

FAITH

Maybe spirit your body away
for objectivity's sake, independence from space,

aggravation for speed, for everything
cannot evaporate into light—still

above us in slow leaps from star
to star, the Devil pulls whole planets

apart with tiger claws, with bear teeth,
and names that debris Heaven.

This we understand when we look
into a telescope and pretend to see anything

but black, everything vanished
like stones behind the river

of skeletons, jumbled and upside down
up there where everything is hideous.

There is a sleek silver scar in the sky,
and isn't it beautiful as long as it's invisible.

We can step off the moon and fall
into a lake. We can step out of the lake

and into the world, out of the world
and know precisely where we will be.

ADEEBA SHAHID TALUKDER

GOD

What feeble minds have held you between their fingers? Despite
your reshapings and growths and falls Manhattan's still living
between banks.

your tide-fist's swell
spread calm as water,
as light, light, light.

Nothing moved between the skins of earth and sky. They sank
into the darkness, traced each other's noses as though it were
love.

the soft of dusk
its waist of light

how much of you moon?
how many eyes the night?

TINA CHANG

EASTER

The F train moves slowly on Sunday and no one
knows the presence of God in the flickering light,
except the woman in a violet dress, hushed into
a lovely bruise, a long stalk of willows in her arms.

No one knows the moment God chooses
to come in the form of Chinese characters
raining down the pages of a book, gently held
by the man sitting next to me.

Twins sit across from me, two Indian men
dressed in matching blue uniforms, whispering
something of their simultaneous unease. Duplicate
voices, siamese cadence. No one knows the time,

the hour of when and where we're rushing.
The windows of the train have been cracked
with stones or with fists. The criss-crossing
pattern of silver tape masks the damage

like a blister, a star. We are populating
a civilization, singing into the air,
as if into the ear of someone great
or anyone who will listen.

MATTHEW OLZMANN

PRAYER NEAR A FARM BY BLACK MOUNTAIN, NORTH CAROLINA: 11:36 PM EARLY MAY

Our Father, who art in
heaven and also
the centipede grass and the creek
and the engine that warbles
roadside: thank you
for the black
silhouette of mountains,
deep black
against the regular black
of the night. Thank you
for the field between me
and them
even though I can't see it.
And thanks for the ability to imagine
what can't be seen.
I imagine you
just as these lowing cows
must have faith in the field
as they glide across it
seeing nothing out here
but the outlines of each other,
my headlights,
an obliterated barn in the distance.

OLIVER DE LA PAZ

AUBADE WITH CONSTELLATIONS, SOME HORSES, AND SNOW

Before dawn the horse-air spools
in the cold. The constellations mimic breaths
fading in their zeroes. This year's worn out
with lusts and grievances passing
from muzzles, vaporizing with Orion.

The house lights in the hills look
to be God with its windows all golden and heroic.

The little mouths of foals at pasture
snuffle for short tufts of grasses splitting ice.
Under stars they snort their own arcs of smoke.

Their coats are gritty and mean. God, they think, is leaning
his shoulder against their flanks,
letting them dream of hay bales and stable doors
unhinged into the liquory dark of evening.

Their helices of in-breath tick,
whole owls of flame. The field turns
like naphthalene—skins and snow.

Light leaves only the glittery skirts of white banks
clouding fence posts. Not memory,
though horses live in both worlds and forgive us.

Sweetness. The mind come again with its arcs of sight:
the man come down from the eye of heaven,
singing *pasture, pasture,* a handful of sugarcubes.

Then the sound of gravel kicked into a truck's stomach . . .
then the clop of hoof on grass as if to say *here is heaven.*
Thus the horses forgive, though they look above.

Whorls of stars like thumb prints on glass. Winter's hard
romances airing out in sleep names. Ear twitch.
They waltz in their sleep to these names. Clover and Hyssop.

Names like tracks of serious foals nudging the ground till dawn
or the breath behind their ear saying *simmer, hush*.

Hoof-prints pour down like color in dream while the nightjars sing
to all the young horses of oatseed, brushes, and troughs.
Cold is sweet on windows of the house, leaving crystal skins.

Dust in the eyes and half out of mind, the horses tremble.
Shapes bent low, re-tracing steps for food. It is their way of keeping
    time—
munching forth the dead into air. Soon the sun will snuff out
the field like dust of a hand. One clump of grass
flat like the shore of another world. One star left snapped
like a beautiful fever. One breath like desire
rocked into the ghost of apples.

PURVI SHAH

IN THE 21ST CENTURY, MIRA REMARKS — KRISHNA'S WAYS OF LOVING BELONG
IN A PARALLEL UNIVERSE

And when you promise me your heart,   will you banish   the flock

of cowherders, the bevy of skirts & dangling chains

                                                which traipse
                                                        in your shadow?

                                                                          the ample heart

            I am still

learning how the wide chest broadens, how

can find its own edges, squeeze
thin borders against lung & ribs, this universe

Such allowance for love is not as natural as crawling
                of opening, remaking & mortaring a room
                                for blossoming.

its music over many others — sometimes as hymn, sometimes
                cr even singing, though
                        we prize

as dirge, sometimes as sometimes —
                        the whisper

barely heard.

            What awaits you?

Reach in then and grab hearth but first
                        jettison flute
                              we both

lest

meet sorrow before each other,
                        the wind of night & sigh

Purvi Shah

of branches beginning

to drip dew, beginning

to shake with wettening

exhilaration. This universe

is ready. Tell me —

are you?

CRAIG SANTOS PEREZ

(DEAR FU'UNA)

~

gi tinituhon : *in the beginning* fu'una transforms her brother
puntan's back into tano' : *land*, chest into langet : *sky*, eyes into
atdao : *sun* and pulan : *moon* // then her breath blooms the odda'
: *soil* and acho' tasi : *coral* \\ then she dives into the place [we]
will name humåtak bay // then her body calcifies into the stone
from which [we] were born \\ laso fu'a : *creation point*

~

first nana : *mother,*
this is my first prayer
to you, full of
wonder // taotao
manu hao : *where*
are you from \\
what made you leave
your first guma' : *home* //
so many of [us] have left
      guåhan
for military and school,
jobs and hospitals \\
forgive me, i lost
our fino' haya : *first*
language in transit, ghost
words // who'll translate
me to you \\ i clutched
my passport aboard
i batkon aire : *the air*
boat to san francisco //
what did you carry
aboard i sakman :
the outrigger canoe \\

Craig Santos Perez

how did you let
go

SUN YUNG SHIN

PAPAVER SOMNIFERUM

The last white tyger

    Surfs from one dreamer to the next

        Reels over each human encampment

Even a colony of one

    I have built her a white poppy field

    I will bury everything to keep Tyger alive

        Hypnos, Nyx, Thanatos

Black as my hand's shadow, bird at rest

        Untaught with a scepter

          Thorns grow backward in this field

The root-world, the under-dream

    Let us walk this neural archipelago

        Leave your shoes in the white wake

Tyger pays no mind

      To my Eden

      Lingua Diablo

        You are no longer ours

        God said

        Said god

        Now you fit to him

      Now you carry his signal like a child

Tune your jaw

    Inward

        Where time waits and grows fur

100 days

Your animal titanimal, serial epithelial

A golden field of sheaves of sleep

Or coiled, bud like a fist

Or an eye

A pale tyger in every bruised flower

The size of trust

A dream is a series of scales

You, your face like a poppy

Bright, enter the center

ED BOK LEE

BOX OF PERSONAL GODS

As a child I slept in a box of prayers,

Each night containing a slightly different problem sent far away
like a pathogen.

In another world they by now must constitute an entire otherly
being, a hideous creature

Surrounded by hinges and smashed lids, rusty and diseased.

One day I hope that monstrosity stomps back in search of me;
demands

To know in which box I hoarded my purest laughter.

In which box have I locked each unopened state of grace.

In which box ferment all those loveliest of human scents.

Of course, I expect, it will curse my extended hands; order me to
go back and revise every last label on my ancestors' good
deeds and sins.

And when I am so old I can only sing sweetly at its menace, may
that it foist upon me a final, largest box

Full of mountains, trees, a river, and four horizons, then lay me
down.

My dear, if only you'd paid more attention, it will whisper, amid a
kaleidoscope of turbulent visions. *There is no immensity after this one.*

But, I'll know: even the oldest box buried deep inside me has
infinity between each face.

SOFIA M. STARNES

BAPTISM OF DESIRE

By way of longing, winter has its eye
on red wings negotiating timber limbs,
blood-rose and tailwind from the winter
bird: and nowhere nest, and nowhere

rest for saints. This I would see and call it
my concern. But only if I'd cradled her;
her feathers tufting, eager to be spared—
and nowhere nest, and nowhere rest

for beasts. Apocalyptic is too long a sigh,
the evening light translates to evening
wind. Again, an eye on whirled and wintered
bird. Awareness is the proper name for nest.

Restless we live; a penknife scrapes a ply-
wood, hinges harp; thud is the shutter's
grim reminder that it shakes. The world's alert
to feelings and to flukes. Until, confessed,

we hunger for the birds.

VIJAY SESHADRI

IMAGINARY NUMBER

The mountain that remains when the universe is destroyed
is not big and is not small.
Big and small are

comparative categories, and to what
could the mountain that remains when the universe is destroyed
be compared?

Consciousness observes and is appeased.
The soul scrambles across the screes.
The soul,

like the square root of minus 1,
is an impossibility that has its uses.

BRYNN SAITO

SHADOW AND RELEASE

Wanting to get clear on her god-thinking, she went out into
that meadow again—golden yarrow and sweetgrass undulating
like a dry sea. She lay down under the sun, which tilted toward
the setting point, but shone brightly. Reeds rose around her;
finches made their dusk songs in steady rhythms. In the tremble
and buzz, she felt the warm wind brush her skin, surprising
her body—ankles, upper neck, belly. When she closed her eyes,
she felt someone's hand slip into hers, their fingers in a cradle,
a full intertwine. Against all of her instincts she didn't turn her
head; she didn't open her eyes. Who is the one who has reached
across to her? Sometimes, the hand felt like her mother's—thin,
powerful—sometimes like the hand her father offered when
she was small and scared, unable to stop her crying in the dark.
Sometimes, the feeling was the feeling she used to have when
lying beside her love in that Brooklyn apartment, their hands
clasped and their hips aligned and their faces pointed totally
away from each other as they fell into sleep. In the meadow-field,
she could feel the curtain of night coming on and the winds
moving in big blue sweeps around her body. She held on, and
something held on to her. When she opened her eyes, she saw no
one.

AMY UYEMATSU

THE OLDER,
THE MORE

"ishigokoro": the "heart" or "mind" of the rock

"Years, months, days, and hours are nothing but the
mind."
  –Dogen, 13th-century Japan

. . . .

lately I feel I belong
to a mind so big—

                many calling it sacred .
                others, love
                or breath

or love and breath and their unending need
                to go on

. . . .

the more I spend time with trees
or stones the more

                I'm certain

of tree mind, stone mind
                complex as my own

. . . .

take a tree, for instance
like the desert willow
                I just planted

surely it knows
                    the violent upheaval
                    from one pot to the next

surely it carries

                    the centuries its ancestors
                    flourished in distant soil

look, three new buds
                    about to explode

part pink, part purple

                    so surely attentive

. . . .

some days I am struck
with the half-open

                    fragments
                    my world
                    moored in paradox

and yet
so many cues

                    whether a small perfect pebble
                    catching my eye

or that small truth
I stumble on, promise

                    not to forget
                    our connections

. . . .

Amy Uyematsu

is this one encompassing mind
or is our starlit galaxy
                        to be found

in the incomparable particulars

my brief seven decades
                        dizzying
                        while still deliberate

and unexpected

                        pine trees
                        black stones
                        white rice

new poems

. . . .

the sky makes it obvious
just follow the clouds

                        infinite mind
                        shifting

between turbulence, calm

no wonder I watch
                        so closely
                        now

and feel so at home

WHO WILL PRAY FOR ME WHEN YOU ARE GONE?: RELATIONSHIPS WITH CULTURAL HISTORY AND ANCESTORS

JENNIFER KWON DOBBS

HOW TO EAT YOUR LOVE

우리 엄아 애게 | *for Omma*

In your version, I come back deformed / a ghost, turned backward

bare feet, decayed teeth / raiding our ancestors' tombs, meat stripped

mouse bones thrown at your door. So you bow your head

stud the boiling red with white knuckles / of young radish as I lick

the lock unable to cross / a rope of chili peppers announcing

your son's birth. The eldest I was a secret / vessel of your rage—

all digestion, I clenched and uncoiled across your pelvis

seizing the greasy bits / you scraped

portioned by the textile factory's canteen. The machines

cranked and thrust. Spitting they fingered every orifice

looped into fresh skein a dark thread / you cursed. *If only it would*
   slide out

For whom do I interpret this fury? *Forgive me*, you say

I was poor, alone / In the economic miracle we were all raw

material, orphaned to fetch / hard currency

like Jeolla-do girls groomed for kisaeng tours, now birth

mothers to the missing crated overseas to military allies

The North reports of a child sold to a New York circus

Let me see my father, Kim Il Sung! she pleads

from the cage / of wire-nosed American greed. I don't believe that

my colleague Cho translated the adopted boy

calling 아저씨, 도와주세요 / *Uncle, help me go home!*

to the white parents carrying him into the Texas Denny's

Jennifer Kwon Dobbs

Eat to remember / to forget each other eat

the charred flesh / lettuce parcels / of conscripted uncles

night-delivered from Vietnam, shrouded in flags / Open your mouth

to the unreliable ones hidden in Russian snow, camptown princesses

"dust of the streets" mixed and nameless / they searched

restaurant scraps as kin to you / a farm girl squatting

to push out contaminants making you sick

Clogged toilet shared by eight families / slabbed cold on the dorm
    floor

All that waste / the factory churned into the river

somehow cleaned blood out of your best cotton dress

Your image struts on stage / righteous and full as

S performs a defector eating rice / evening KBS / nuclear threat

absorbed as nutrients / Her body radiates like a transmitter

slogans I heard in Pyeongyang / a parked truck blaring unity songs

during morning rush hour / She eats with precision the ghosts

of her amputation / A scripted regime / collapse produces bodies

mute, grim, consuming / shades / where the missing

limbs can still be felt / Here, Omma, you claim a summons

to build your prayer house / The fourth wall falls away

Jennifer Kwon Dobbs

Platters of grilled pork, three fish picked apart later / you beat

my shoulders casting out histories locked in the muscle / You entreat

a scar-eyed Jesus to restore my barren womb / You design my
    resurrection

like the military engineers personhood

through syllabi and "great books" / star students

trained in singing / A veteran, the professor reminisced about the head

he buried miles from the Korean soldier's body / Well-intentioned

he ate a cookie while the class studied his photos / I'm supposed to chew

the dead / again and again in effigy / You order me to

go to church to atone for your sins / to forget

because we're "a well-fed nation" / He wrote to the administration

proud of his service, furious at his censure / casting me

out as a woman he could've bought in a camptown / all the
    children

he rescued with chocolate and socks / a bitter orphan who

the generalissimo outfitted with explosives

Untenurable / with slim fingers I could wire a shrapnel storm

You revise me into a functional body / you stuff with duck meat

expensive fruits and kim—bribes so I'll translate your way home

to your baby son / I tire of use but here's my left hand rewriting

this DMZ gorge and purge economy / Who can begrudge you

a 빨리빨리 mise en scène? / So my illiterate brother will remember

you pack suitcases of mountain roots / I'll cook as your surrogate

With each bite his limbs retract into your toddler kidnapped, sent
    away

now craving / And I ring with cartilage반환하는 혼이

a ghost pink and fattening inside my belly / You at last

free from history / O sticky hunger

cut down from the rafters of my dry breasts / New person eating

two into one / You discard the extraneous

girl / hide and scoop up the boy

KHATY XIONG

HIGH GARDEN

The flowers in the garden grow rapidly
as if they are in a hurry to lay eggs or wisdom
or the proper exchange of souls is at stake.
I am wearing a gown, which I never do.
For the occasion that I may see her
in the parade of dying lanterns, sizzling
joss boats and the world's lost medicine.
Tragic, really, is the music coming from the elders
who mop their cheeks with cooperating birds
whose wings grow heavy with crying.
It is typical now but every evening
the car accident is the same and gives me
the same tears. There are no new ones.
She loved carnations, which is true, including
several other flowers. The opium poppy is obvious.
She ate them thrice every morning.
How fresh and responsibly high I imagine
like a queen of the Mekong spitting back
the clothes of the ones who fell into her body
—and what of the flowers' thoughts as they enter
mother's womb and see there is no child?
Everlasting drops of dew and frothy
like a cave of demons who have made arrows
out of the ferns and quite effectively. Scary
in every way. I am being polite now.
As for the dress I never gave it a color.
It is sage and the exact shade of my veins.
Repeatedly I clap my hands then harder
and every light in the sky goes boom.

MIA AYUMI MALHOTRA

TO MY MANY MOTHERS, ISSEI AND NISEI

Praise be to beef liver stew, to gravy biscuits
        and home-baked bread, to women
in work pants and suspenders who *worked like dogs*
        in the packing shed, up to elbows
in rose clippings. You fed us well, O goddesses
        of goulash and green beans, of Sunday dinners
wrangled from the coop. For penny money
        and seamstressing, praise. For parsnips
and sweet potatoes, praise. Even for the years lost
        to sharecropping and strawberries, hallelujah.
You worked until the final hour then rose
        three days later, baby squalling on your hip,
back to breaking canes, clipping hooks,
        hustling the men through lunch hour.
No breaks, boys. Hallelujah to Pond's Cold Cream,
        to curling rags and church bento socials.
Praise to the nursery truck revving in the morning,
        the clank of steel pipes and boiler-
house rumble. All glory to the Berkeley streetcar
        and Key Route electric train, the smokestacks
of Richmond and foggy peaks of San Francisco.
        And because they're what taught us to praise,
glory to the roses run wild, the packing shed
        left to cobweb. Praise to the crowded horse stalls
and half-built barracks of Rohwer, Arkansas,
        dusty sheets and muffled nights of Block 9-9-C,
100. Sakai, Chu. 102. Sakai, Ruby. 103. Sakai, Kazue.
        O praise to the camp midwives, the Nisei girls
shooting hoops and swatting birdies when their mothers
        weren't looking. And to the college-bound coed
who crossed the country, camp release papers
        in hand, hallelujah. Her truth marches on.

K-MING CHANG

TELEVANGELISM

for Agong

In Chinese, *ghost* rhymes
    with *expensive* & mother

misspends her mouth
    on prayer with no payback, no god

bending our sky like a back.
    What a daughter costs

a mother must pay
    out of body: she reaches

into her blood
    like a wallet, a wound

we eat out of. She says
    one man's daughter

is another god's revenge: a river
    lassoes our local church & my body

expires mid-prayer.
    I wear my blood

as bracelets & go sleeveless
    on Sundays. When it rains, I cinch

the flood around my waist
    like a miniskirt. Say we'll be better

mothers than our mothers. Say our fathers fit
    in our fists. When I microwave my mouth

a prayer boils over. My tongue
   tides. Mother heaps a houseful

of salt on our family altar, fills
   a bath & stripteases, teaches me

to do the dead
   man's float. In a church

made of bone, I boil
   a broth of fathers.

I season my wounds
   & wear them aloud, my blood

lungs. I pile salt into an anthill
   & crawl home. When it floods, we flee

on the backs of our brothers. We
   each a queen. We seek sweet

things, eat our stomachs
   starved out & sugared.

Agong dies after dinner, bladder
   come loose like a coin purse, piss

scattering like pennies
   on the bed. Make a wish. Fling

a coin into his mouth & a god comes
   true. Call a river a phoneline, my voice

snipped into silences. There is no country
   where we can afford to bury our dead.

Mourning, too, is an economy
   of light. It was day when he died

& dark when I miscarried a moon
   into the wrong country's night.

We burned paper Chinese
   money & it was the first

time I've seen my face
   on something worth

something. No one tells me
   why we capitalize God

but never ghost.
   Never grieve.

NEIL AITKEN

THE ART OF FORGETTING

How to swim, how to ride a bike– even how to voice
my own name in my mother's tongue, each sound
a hard and pitted salt plum I marry to my teeth,
but cannot break open.

Forgetting is in the blood, something gleaned
from my grandmother—her hate strong enough
to wipe clean the first two years of married life,
the loss of her world, my mother's birth.

When I wake this morning to the grey Taipei sky
and dress in that early light that filters in somehow
through a hundred shades of smog, it is hard to believe
it has been a year already in this home not quite home.

Here, at the gate of memory, I am not my grandmother
grown transparent with age, but rather some lost son come
in stranger's clothes, the air ripe with incense and ash.
I want to remember this year and the one yet to be.

They say that the muscles have memory, that the body recalls
any motion rehearsed over time. An old horse always returns.
Mile after mile, my body relearns Taiwan the hard way—I feel it
when I move, in the way my calves have hardened, in the scar

on my chest where my muscles split wide when a truck door opened
in front of my bike, in the callouses on my knees where I have knelt
every morning on the cement and tile floors and offered a prayer
full of fire and forgetting for someone to come down to loosen my
     tongue,

to unlock that rusted door and let what beats within go free.

HEI KYONG KIM

WATER MASK

How do you find memory when you are born from amnesia?

I settle in a hot tub of water with a ghost mask on my face; a Korean shaman mask of sorts, dripping with chemicals that soften the skin, calling upon agelessness and immortality. The spirits enter and float to the ceiling corners, traditional music blasting from my iPhone that lies on the rugged bathmat. Welcome all. They are quiet because we do not speak the same language and I'm actually no longer listening.

You have no culture...
Do you have a soul, or was it removed in that neglected crib of yours?

A bath tub full of hot water welcomes the ancestors, invites them in the form of boxelder bugs and the kayagum. Sea foam dim expands until I am drifting in a womb, aloneness melts away. I am inside my mother again, this time without worry of being expelled.

My tongue only craves Korean food these days.

The shrill, melancholic song of the ajumma brings me back to a memory of a dream I once had without words—A halmoni in a white hanbok smiled at me and gave me a fan in front of an altar, a mountain in the backdrop. Her smile radiated with warmth and love. She rang a bell that I later found in real time on a table in an empty room by my office. I took it—that was back before I declined her presence and pushed her away.

I am lost without the mask; no one wants to speak to you because you are ugly to them, because you can't find the words to communicate...to connect...to attach.

I am in need of rebirth.

DEBRA KANG DEAN

ADAM'S APPLE

i.

At twenty months my nephew,
having already mastered the sound
of sense, held my attention
as I sliced an apple crosswise
to show him the stars.

After he'd strung three pieces
on his finger then tossed them
on the floor, he shrieked
and kicked and pointed
an insistent finger

elsewhere. Like the dunce
who searched for fire
with a lighted lantern, "Tell me,"
I pleaded, "tell me"
you little Neanderthal.

ii.

The skeleton found at Kebara
made me rethink Neanderthal.

Among the remains a hyoid—
shaped like a wishbone almost

the length of my thumb. Bone?
I press thumb and index finger

against my throat in search
of my own hyoid bone.

The 60,000 years between us contract:
He could speak. And I—

there was a time I couldn't speak.
Some days, loving the lump in my throat

I think of the impulse to name
as Adam's curse, our apple.

iii.

Not the ash, but the bones
are the reason we cremate;
picking through what remains

with chopsticks, we're after
this one, in particular,
Arimoto insists, pointing

at his Adam's apple—
we burn off the flesh,
he says, and fire the bones

just till they break
under their own weight—
nodobotoke, we call it

Buddha in the throat.

CHRISTY NAMEE ERIKSEN

CONGEE

When a parent makes their child soup
they cast a spell over the whole house.

The walls smell the ginger and they stand
taller. The garlic's skin is so thin

it flies away when you talk about it but
it never falls, only flutters, proof

that the kitchen means well.
The freezer is a cold place, but it's

not a lonely one. Anyway I'd make
friends there, before waiting made

me mean. Even a chicken as stubborn
as this one softens when it is touched.

Everything craves purpose.
Child, when you were born

I didn't know if I had enough magic.
Who knows

if I am made of the right things.
But I have tasted

aches and pains and I can
cook them. When the rice simmers

I can hear the roof
repairing itself. I can feel a fever

break.

PREETI KAUR RAJPAL

MAKING ROTI IN THE LANGAR KITCHEN OFF HIGHWAY 99

after my grandmother became

knives sleep the onions and garlic chopped
in cubes of light thrown into the steel pot of daal
a chariot boiling over the room fills with a woman
gaggle discussing death and dough lies
in front of us a beached whale our heads
covered in cloth like prayer i pinch off atta
roll small balls in my hands pass them to other
women a line of slapping flipping rolling flattening
throwing onto the gas flame the room blue
in hum of someone else's grandmother overseeing
stacks of hundreds of round roti to feed the hungry
living guests on a saturday close to cremation

we say in life a person is adhoora
only part of themselves a person
becomes poora whole when they leave
return into the circling a steel bracelet
around our pulsing wrists

here in the langar kitchen a small girl
rubs butter on steaming rotis like i used to
learning the ways of being with blood
her long hair in braids like ropes through time

in the corner a lucky man on asylum his turban
loose with work stirring the vat of milk with a wooden
oar reciting god's name to shroud us from curdling
peddling us through this thickening world of living neither
here nor there his thumb a stub singed with boiling
all the police left when the blades awake the men disappearing

from punjab's countryside
like bread

JOSEPH O. LEGASPI

SKETCHES FROM A CHILDHOOD SEA

> "… the sea is a continual miracle, / … What
> stranger miracles are there?"
> **–Walt Whitman**

I was born surrounded.

*

Scroll down map. Manna.
My first glimpse of the archipelago.

Directive finger pointed at the dispersal,
god-thundered *Here*, brown islands
breaking up blue parchment
like a birthmark.

*

My tiny toes tickled by tropical sand,
I faced a roaring power, charging relentlessly
but unable to reach me. Great strength
and its limits.

Yet, drawn,
I refused to be brave against a great rapture.

*

Pacific Ocean. South China Sea. Babuyan Channel. Strait of
    Luzon.
Mindoro Strait. Bohol Sea. Sulu Sea. Celebes Sea. Philippine—.

*

We are not separated by water, rather connected by it.

*

My uncles each grabbed a limb—legs and arms—I feared being torn apart. A frog pinned as an asterisk in science class, ready for the scalpel. Then swung like a hammock until released into the monstrous mouth of the ocean. What they taught the city boy
    was how to flail.

*

I loved the briny taste of me. Sea salt crusted on my lips, skin.
The outrigger canoe at sunrise, haul of the nets ornamented like
    Christmas.

*

Through the screen of urban night I try to envision the sea.

It is there, waves like sonar. Traveling hushed yet vibrating as
    underwater.

My mother was my original sea. I was divine, then microscopic.

I outgrew, turned into raft, boat, yacht.

How do I remain saline?

*

Before I was born
the world existed.

(Imagine.)

I was set aside:
one cell,

ocean reconfigured.

The depths roused
my animal life.

Crawled.

Horseshoe crab with its
shell of chitin.

Before consciousness
ships had sailed
across histories.

*

I was then moved to the other end of the Pacific.

*

As I flew over it, on an American plane,
I reminisced of the summers shrimping
in the tributaries, of fishing boats laden
with lobsters and sun-golden men,
of the time I bicycled over a toad,
flattened on my hurry to the sea.

CRAIG SANTOS PEREZ

(DEAR FU'UNA)

~

in the past, our ancestors pilgrimaged each year to laso fu'a //
they made offerings and asked blessings for *simiya* : seed, hale' :
root, and talaya : *net* \\ they stood in circles and chanted rhymed
verses back and forth // [we] call this communal poetic form
kåntan chamorrita (which translates as *to sing both forwards and
backwards*)

~

first nana,
were you pregnant
when you labored
through contracting
waves and dilating
horizons // could you
feel [us] paddling
within as you walked
to humåtak bay \\
were you scared
to give birth in this
new place // were you
worried about [us]
being safe here

~

the spanish brought their god and bible, suppressed the story of
fu'una and puntan, and forbade the procession to laso fu'a in
humåtak bay

CRAIG SANTOS PEREZ

(DEAR PUNTAN)

~

as a patgon : *child*, i never heard the creation story of our first
mother, fu'una (whose name translates as *first*), or our first *father*,
puntan (whose name translates as *coconut sapling*) // grandma
always said "in the beginning was the word and the word was
god

~

first tata : *father*
this is my first prayer
to you, full of questions //
what was your father's name
\\ where is he buried //
          what song maps
did he teach you
before crossing ocean
// when you planted
the first coconut sapling
here, when its roots pushed
through husk into soil,
did you feel belonging \\
          you sacrificed
your known world
so that [we] will inherit
shelter // is this
what it means to be
a father

EILEEN R. TABIOS

MAGANDA BEGINS

"Maganda" is not just a Tagalog word that means "beautiful."
"Maganda" is also the name of the first woman in a Filipino
creation myth.

My love. If
words can
reach

whatever world you
suffer in—
Listen:

I have things
to tell
you.

At this muffled
end to
another

year, I prowl
somber streets
holding

you—in my
head, this
violence!—

a violent gaze.
You. With
dusk

arrives rain drifting
aslant like

premature

memory. Am I
the one
who

suddenly cleared these
streets? *My*
Love,

all our hours
are curfew
hours—

what I offer
is this
dying

fish into whose
gullet I
have

thrust my thumb.
Why did
you

lose all Alleluias?
My love—
Listen:

SAHAR MURADI

TIMBUKTU

Salaam alaikum
Once, when I was a girl

I ni sógóma
I believed in morning,
like a hot, yellow apple

Manda nabasheyn
We never tired. Father said,
God is good

Héré sira
We slept in twos and threes

Famil chatoor ast
It was a matter of everyone

Sómógó bédi
Someone had work, someone didn't
Someone always offered something

Owlada khoob astan
We were kids but we knew everything
We belonged to everyone

I sigi na
After prayer, there was tea
After tea, there was fruit

Befarmayen
Mother taught us to draw our feet
To let others go first

Aw ni tile
In time, day gave way to night

Jan e tan jor ast
Someone would show up asking for my body
Then another

I dógó cé ka kéné
We would exchange brothers
who were not our brothers

Khudaya shukur
The earth met us in different ways
For some, it rained
For others, there wasn't water for the stones

A barika Allah ye
We thanked God for blessing us
and not our neighbors

Khuda hafez
History was the first to leave
and without a trace

Aw ni wula
Father said the night has hands
Mother reminded me of the apple

Shab bakhair
In the dark
I held nothing

TARFIA FAIZULLAH

ACOLYTE

The white cross pales
further still,
            its nailed arms
watchful as window-light

furls over the backs of our knees,
as lavender shadows
            cut across
our young necks

in this makeshift classroom
church where I kneel with
            the others, restless
on the cracked leather

kneeler—how I crave
these cream candles,
            how my hungry
tongue sings

fidelis, fidelis
as I imagine Mother
            in her kitchen
humming
black and white

film songs as she curls
her hennaed fingers
            around the rolling pin's
heavy back and forth

while Father rocks
in his chair, the Qur'an
            on his desk open to the last
page, the dark words

blurring as his eyes close,
seeing again the shapla-flower
            shaped epitaph

Tarfia Faizullah

on his father's

tombstone. Now, with my head
bowed, I whisper *amar*
     naam Tarfia until it is
a prayer that grows.

I help stack the hymnals
higher, and
cup the candlelight away.

VANDANA KHANNA

ELEPHANT GOD

If I was a good Hindu, I would believe
as my mother does—that ashes sprinkled
in the Potomac River will somehow reach

the Ganges—that my father, reborn,
is somewhere in the world, someone else's
husband, father. Or maybe I have it all wrong

and he is a daughter, not Indian or Hindu,
just living in a cold city near a river that flows back
upon itself. I am waiting for a sign, like you

calling from Delhi to say the wooden elephants
are drinking goat's milk. All over the country, people
spoon it into tusks and mouth. The milk's slow trickle

cracking thick skin, the wood brittle as teeth, blessed,
ready to snap. And it's something like religion—behind
carved wood, ivory tusks, there is something

drinking, someone listening to prayers with milk. I wait
for the day a postcard left in my mailbox will say
"Yes I am here, it is wonderful." Every hang up

on my answering machine is him calling
over and over just for the need to say
he is somewhere in the world. I will ask,

"Is the river really that color of night?" and whisper
words in my childhood tongue, something like *Ram, Ram,*
something like *make me holy*.

VANDANA KHANNA

HINDU MYTHOLOGY IN SHORTHAND

It begins with the blue god—master
of charm, flute, and cows.

Then the holy monkey who
thrashes through the jungle

crushing everything lush and green
underfoot. I'm seven and can't sleep

because it's not Virginia, it's not
snowing. The stories are all

in Sanskrit, in Hindi—jumbled
and cloudy in my ears. My grand-

mother wants me to forget it's
Christmas in India. She tells

of Durga riding a tiger, arms
filled with sickles and swords:

vindication manifest in steel's
sharp edges. Of stolen Sita

selfless and pure, the sag of
her mud-streaked sari I imagined

the color of unused sky, green
of Himalayan summers

but it was probably red, like every
other one I'd seen since I'd gotten

off the airplane—shades of crimson
shades of bleeding. There was

that smell—Delhi?—that I couldn't
sniff out of my nose: incense and

sandalwood, husked corn and lemons
the tar of oily streets and burning

tires following me through
road-side stalls and halal markets

down rows of henna and biscuits
caught in the crease of my neck

in the bucket of bath water, on
the cotton pillow sown with tiny

mirrors reflecting back bits of
myself. Then the holy charioteers

with blazing arrows pinned the sky
with fire, and we sang *OM* and

Ram, Ram me trying to make it
sound like it was born in my mouth

my third eye still awake behind
the skull's delicate cradle, blinking.

AMY UYEMATSU

PILGRIMAGE TO JOKHANG TEMPLE

April, 2013

1

Here in Lhasa the sky
is brighter, a truer blue
at 12,000 feet high.

2

Outside the temple I can't stop watching
the pilgrims prostrate themselves—
some using mats, others falling
to the hard concrete sidewalk,
crawling on hands and knees.

How patiently they stand in line,
after waiting a lifetime to kneel before
the Jowo Shakyamuni, the holy statue
of Buddha. Many spin prayer wheels,
smile at me with shining eyes.

3

On surrounding streets
small units of eight to ten
Chinese soldiers march
armed with guns
and fire extinguishers.

Last year two young monks
set themselves ablaze—
self-immolation, a modern legacy
shared with farmers and nuns,
parents and schoolchildren.

Amy Uyematsu

4

The pilgrims drape long white scarves
around their shoulders and necks.
They will lay these scarves at the altar,
along with thermoses and pitchers
filled with yak butter from farms.

5

Our guide warns us not to aim
cameras in the soldiers' direction.
He's not allowed to tell how the Red Guards
housed here in the sixties burned
hundreds of ancient scriptures.

I have so many questions
the guide can't answer.

6

Without speaking the pilgrim's language,
I recognize a spiritual devotion unfamiliar
to me. Is the ardor that burns within them
stronger because of war, more fervent
because their Dalai Lama was forced to leave?

Or is this yearning born from something deeper,
their long history of suffering sustained by
a faith I may never understand,
a sacred practice unaffected by political winds—
ancient and enduring as Tibet.

JOSEPH O. LEGASPI

GRACE

The carabao arrived on our street bearing the world,
pulling a wooden cart hill-high with watermelons.
Its handler, a man the rich color of coffee, tugged

at the driving line, a rope tied through the septum
circumnavigating master and beast. Seated beside
the man was his son, a mocha version of himself.

As I was, paler than my mestizo father, who met
the melon sellers with our neighbors, lured by cool
promise of relief from the tropic's audacious heat.

Outer gentleman, watermelon lover, my father
scanned the stacked pyramid, held up a dull fruit,
palmed the creamy, yellow underbelly, weighted it

cupped in his all-knowing, all-punishing hands.
Next, a gentle knock, like he'd do before entering
their bedroom restless past midnight. His knuckles

bounced off the bell-domed curve, he listened, eyes
closed, and, as he is dead now, for years, he longed
for that sonorous sound echoing inside the dense

watery ripeness. I watched him then, as I always did,
man of eternal theater, of elegant fingers, this Lazarus
figment memory I call poetry, my father full of grace.

DUY DOAN

PRAYER IN WRITING

When I pray, I often pray to Bà Ngoại.
When I write, I always have in mind a living reader.
When I pray, I pray for myself.
When I write, it's the same.

I've prayed to Bà that she pray for me.
I've prayed to God to help me pray genuinely.

I write in symbol:
committing the unforgivable sin, I adulterate prayer with metaphor,
asking God to make me less like Jacob, and more like Esau.
But in praying this,
I become Jacob.

When I pray, I shouldn't use words.
When I write, I shouldn't use prayer.
I should write as I pray.
Or I should stop writing.

MARIANNE CHAN

DECEMBER 1998

You are dreaming of a brown Christmas
with people who have never trusted

snow. Christmas begins on the guitar,
and ends on the windowsill

where your uncles
in your father's hand-me-down t-shirts

lean on their elbows until early morning.
Here, the windows have no glass,

protect no secrets. This year, you ask
Santa Claus for an alarm clock

to keep you awake because you don't
want to shut your eyes

to the stringed lights on the banana leaves,
the paper lanterns dangling from houses,

fall on your knees, oh hear—
Perhaps, Santa is your drunken uncle

imparting wisdom, beating his neighbors
at chess, eating miniature green bananas,

lounging on reclining lawn furniture
with his open shirt, in his wide open

living room, yelling for his children—who
are older than you but smaller—to come

inside and eat. Or, Santa is your

mother who arrived on the islands

from a German America in the middle
of the night holding her groggy children

(you) in her arms, making an entrance
with luggage filled with canned goods,

underwear, and lethargy. To the balikbayan,
loneliness is given in return. A desire to leave

after remembering the melancholic taste
of ripe lansones on the lips, how

your grandfather died before he met snow,
and how your grandmother lost

her legs to disease. *Fall on your knees, oh hear*
the heart quiver on the stringed instruments.

Still her ghost lingers, her legs reattached
by death. On these islands, white Christmas

is a play on words. Santa exists in theory.
But the dead exist in practice.

On the dining table, leave mangos for the dead,
rice, a plate of chocolate. Then, when all

is quiet, listen for footsteps on the roof
of their house, and do not shut your eyes.

E. J. KOH

FATHER IN HIS OLD AGE

There is a Korean belief that you are born
the parent of the one you hurt most. Watching
my father use chopsticks to split chicken katsu,
he confesses that I may be the reincarnation
of his own father. We finished our waters in silence
and walked home chatting about who to blame
for where we are. He says, *The present is the revenge
of the past.* Revenge goes too far, I argue. And
in our unhappiness, we both want to know
we cannot pay enough. Pain becomes meaning.
After this life, I fear I'll never meet him again.

MONICA SOK

SONG OF AN ORPHANED SOLDIER CLEARING LAND MINES

When I saw my father walking I kicked the road,
convinced metal brains at his feet
the humming they heard was a knife cutting,
not a living man's voice.
They believed me. Like snakes in grass
they clicked their tongues. The gods I met
promised me they could make a life happen
after what had happened
if I knew who my father was.
I clapped my hands to signal a stream
and my father followed my sound.
He drank and bathed as I cleared the land mines
and I hoped it was him. He slept
in the jungle, dreamed jaguars circling
though it was nothing but fire burning.

Close to the Bassac, I climbed mango trees
to feed him. Along the way,
I waved my arms *no*. To himself my father said, *Yes*.
No, I did not bury the bodies
nobody had prayed for. There are things in this world
we must make one another see. My father
took me gently, each one of us
gently, he took us to the flames humming *my children,
my children*. Three provinces, I traveled with him
like this, only to take him back to Prek Eng
where he found his sisters.

If my father were to tell this, he would tell you
he carried me over his shoulders to a nearby village,
that no danger touched him
and that the gods were watching,
they wanted to see me live.

SU HWANG

CANCER

Feet on dashboard, god-awful music blaring from mixed
cassettes, my father let me have my way as he played

chauffeur, never easing his grip on the wheel down straightaways.
Four hours to my college dorm across New Jersey and the Poconos,

up through Scranton to the gulch of Broome County in upstate
New York, not a word passed between us, mile after

mile markers on fence posts, yellow dashes, streaks of trees—
blurred liturgy of autumn, spring. Summer into winter into

summer, ticking off hours that measured the distance as he drove
and I watched the road that held nothing but our widening gulf.

My father taught me willful reticence, folding desire
into cellular spaces. Perhaps one day I will enter this dusty

warehouse filled with neglected boxes, find the one labeled
For My Daughter, and unpack its long-held secrets. For now, I let

him seal their seams with tape, stuff them into corners. Recently
when I visited, he sat across the dinner table as Mom prepared

our holiday meal, both of them aging exponentially like radioactive
particles. Wisp of his former self, barely recognizable, recited

the Lord's Prayer: *Our father in heaven, hallowed be your name,*
your kingdom come, your will be done, on earth as it is in heaven.

They had just taken out his kidney: the half. *Life of*
failure. Suddenly he opened his eyes, looked straight into me,

and said, *I know you. You have a frontier spirit.* Where did he even get that word: *frontier*. We nodded in agreement, then ate in

silence like we always do, losing our nerve. All I've ever wanted
him to say is: Tell me something. Tell me—everything.

MARIANNE CHAN

ORIGIN STORY

1.

Not Eve, but Eve's Filipino half-sister, bad dancer, lute player, naked and fat, fermenting grains, painting veins with berries and clay, shoots the shit with snake and tree beneath moonlight, while God, Eve, and even Adam make fires in caves, drawing pictures of buffalo and horses on walls, like a bunch of wacko, hallucinating tunnel dwellers.

2.

"When you were born," my mother tells me, "You resembled our statue of Buddha." Not the thin icon, not the skeletal, ascetic Siddhartha Gautama, but Pu-Tai, the fat one in American Chinese restaurants, symbol of abundance and generosity. She says: "You always drank too much soda. Your father gave you whatever you wanted, even if it wasn't good for you. That is why you were happy." Hedonism is not natured, but nurtured. As she finishes telling me this, she stretches her stout body along the loveseat in her newly bought suit. She burps after her snack of fried chicken. She asks me to rub her feet while she watches *Jeopardy!*, and then, she offers to rub mine.

3.

Not Eve, but Eve's serpent, imbibing fruit juices and writhing her leggy body on the branch of a tree. I always imagined that the serpent had the legs of a seductive woman in black nylons before God took them away as punishment. Maybe she wanted them to go. She wanted to feel the earth, her origin, warm on her belly. Where are the legs now? Perhaps, at the bottom of the ocean, alongside the remains of the Ark, a pair of ancient nylons is steadily disintegrating.

4.

"When you were born," my father tells me, "you looked just like I did." He hands me a black-and-white picture of himself in a crib, a weeping baby. How pleasurable it is, as a child, to instantly find your origins in some earlier being. The future is predestined. I see my eyes in his eyes, his crooked gait in my crooked gait. I look up at my father. I think: In a few years, I will be a sixty-year-old Chinese man with a black-and-white mustache.

5.

Not Eve, but eve. Before my father was my father's father, a man who had twenty children with numerous women, a man who drank and smoked and did not wish to die. Before my mother was my mother's mother, a woman who lost her legs, like the wonderful, wise serpent who initiated life and earthly joys. Eve. The day that comes before an important day. A name given after shame. My brother tells me that when I was born I had a mark on my head that resembled a tree, and it grew fruit until it disappeared. That's a myth. The truth of the story: after us, there will be another, then another, then another.

FAISAL MOHYUDDIN

THE OPENING

> "It is You we worship; it is You we ask for help. Guide us on the straight path: the path of those You have blessed, those who incur no anger and who have not gone astray."
>
> **–The Holy Quran, "Al-Fatiha,"**
> **verses 5-7**

THE CHILD: Tell me, Father,
what new turbulence took hold
in your blood on the day of my birth,
and did your stomach sink
each time I cried out for the basket
of your arms?

THE FATHER: I held you too close
to feel anything but the wild
gallop of your tiny heart.

THE CHILD: Did you recite
the call to prayer in my ear, slip
your pinky, dipped in honey, in my mouth
to mark with song and sweetness
my entry into the ummah
of the Prophet Muhammad,
peace be upon him?

THE FATHER: All night, I nursed
a candle's flame, leaning in and out
of its sphere of light, mumbling verses
of the Qur'an, mispronouncing
the Arabic, not understanding a word
beyond "Al-Fatiha," but knowing,
nonetheless, I had fulfilled
this first obligation of fatherhood.

THE CHILD: What was it like
to look into my eyes for the first time?

THE FATHER: I felt as if my fingers
had combed the embryonic silt feathering
the deepest bottom of the ocean.
And when I resurfaced, holding the key
to fatherhood, I understood
the true worth of being a living thing.

THE CHILD: What did you say
to Mother when she could not find
the words to tell you about how
the breaking open of a body
propels one toward heaven, that God
promises the greatest share of Paradise
to mothers?

THE FATHER: After a long silence,
I said, "To every unutterable thing
buried in your heart, to every miraculous truth
teetering on the tip of your tongue,
yes, yes, *ameen*."

THE CHILD: Did you spill the blood
of two goats, give their meat to the poor,
to bless my arrival, to mark
the transition of my soul
from the library of the eternal
into the living fire of a body too fragile to share?

THE FATHER: For twenty years,
I harvested the silhouette of my father's voice
from the night sky, let its echo rock me
to sleep whenever I felt so crushed
by heartache that even God's infinite love,
a rescue vessel sailing through a history
of bloodshed and loss, could not hold me

intact enough to believe in survival—
so if it was my hand or another's
that guided the blade along two throats
I cannot recall, nor do I want to.

THE CHILD: What else
might you have done
had fatherhood not stolen you
from the life you knew?

THE FATHER: When a surgeon
saves your life by amputating a limb
housing a reservoir of poison,
you do not curse the violence
of his work, nor the pain of the procedure.
You bow down before God,
You thank the man, you learn to write
with the other hand, to walk
on one leg.

THE CHILD: One final question,
Father. What should I say
when my son, when I too become a father,
asks me about the hours
of your life that exist beyond
my knowing?

THE FATHER: Tell him more
about the hours of your life
so his hunger is not as desperate
nor as bottomless
as ours.

RAJIV MOHABIR

WHALE STORY

I. Matsya

> "And having sat thusly, I will guide you across the oceans."
> **–Vishnu in "Krishna" by Ramanand Sagar**

It's not my fault demons
        steal Vedas from your mouth
as you sleep. If you forget
            your prayers will you float?

Breathing air I come
        to point out the moon. Don't pack
grains for this voyage.
            Pack folksongs. If you capsize

your lungs will seize up,
        catch fire of salt and sputter.
All about you ghost arms
            of drowned men try

to submerge you, beg you to cool
        their tongues white
with hunger. Their fired
            iron and steel hooks,

will scald your skin
        like undying sun.
Tie your vessel to my horn
            and offer garlands

to the sea, your own name
        a mantra to the god
of exile, the ruler of life.

One day your children

will crack coconuts,
            grind chutney from the tropics'
plankton bloom, and beckon
                        demons to their gold.

II. Cetus

Andromeda,
It's wise to hallucinate
as you await the beast
that will devour you.
The cetacean's a storm
whose eye withstands
the pressure of diving
nose first into the abyss.
Because of pride
the innocent are chained
to rocks and sacrificed.
Even if you survive
betrayal by your mother
to the sea-god, how
could you possibly return
home? Your patria
will strip away your caste.
Or perhaps a savior
with skin like a ghost
will smite the whale
into mere phantasm.
You are obsessed with
reentering the womb
once its spits you out;
there's no return from
exile so why not destroy
every beauty?

III. Bake-kujira

Imagine, a wraith—beautiful
and terrible—
rises from the brine.

It's the skeleton of a baleen
whale whalers shoot with iron hooks.

A phantom in calcium,
spears pass through its queer apparition

which is picked to the ghost.
O god of bone,

is it micro-plastic, the hunt,
or radiation that causes
you to rise up from the grave,

to unsettle rivers and tide, harrowing
and intent on prophecy?

Fish and birds, warped and
misshapen
from human carelessness, attend you.

Plastic gouges their guts;
they rot as albatrosses on Midway
and dry conjoined

as grey whales on a Baja beach.

Every living intestine fills with
radioactive nuclides.

O Kujira, forgive me
for lancing your lung with my silence:

an auto-annihilation
from which
none can be revived.

IV. Leviathan

> "Can you fill its hide with harpoons
> or its head with fishing spears?"
> **—Bible: Job 41:7**

O God of Abraham, Isaac, of Jacob,
     I have lanced this monster
through the nose, lassoed its tongue
with rope, and carve its flesh
into the shape of a Bible.

     May your will be done.

     I've seen the sea transform
from coral to crimson, gallons
and gallons of gore frothing
in the thrash of fluke and harpoon;
the final sputter of hellfire.
You crush the mighty heads
with just one blink.

     Your name be praised
as the walls of Jericho
tumble into dust.

O God of eternal resource,
     as I am your servant, give to me
loyal slaves, give to your devoted
always, a black body to spear,
and land thirsty for conquering.

V. Niho Lei Palaoa

'O luna, 'o lalo, 'o uka, 'o kai, 'o ka palaoa pae—no ke
  ali'i ia.
Above, below, the upland, the lowland, the whale that washes
  ashore—all belong to the chief.

Hanau ka Palaoa noho i kai
Born is the Odontoceti living in the sea.
          –Kumulipo

Who controls the palaoa
carved into a tongue
and strung about your neck
with braids of human hair
is true ali'i—a ruler who controlled
the corpses of beached whales.
They posses the tooth-ivory,
this kinolau, this carved palaoa,
one bodily form of sea-god Kanaloa,
giving strength to their speech,
tidal force to their decree.
Yet how can power remain
when today, during RIMPAC
in the bay, American sonar pulses
drive melon-headed whales to scrape
their tonnage against the fringe
reef, bleeding from their ears,
to wither on the sands
of the "most beautiful beach
the world over." I shuffle
my feet in Wakīkī's gold, my skin
roasting its greed. A bleached
coral bites my heel or is it rib
or vertebra? Whose place
have I taken—

along the beach singing one song
tropic birds and pigeons without breath
now white now kea.

VI. Dhan-Nun (Yunus, *sallallahu* wasallam)

> "Then the fish swallowed him, while he was
> blameworthy."
> **–Al-Qur'an 37: 142**

Nothingness thrummed within,
rahimhuallah, may Allah be merciful,

a djin in the heart of the whale.
I begged the seamen, *Heft this body;*

hurl me into the sea. My prayer
a chord of light. But first I must atone;

stomach acid must scald
my skin. I must come

to face dusk, swallowed whole.
I must write the poem

where I admit running away
with the neighbor boy, packing

a bottle of gin and condoms.
I must admit my failures as a son:

I left my father alone,
without an heir; I never used

the condoms. I break my name
in two, -*maha* -*bir*, holding

onto *bir,* the part that means *semen.*

WE WERE BROWN AND IMMIGRANT: SPIRITUAL PRACTICE AS A FORM OF POLITICAL RESISTANCE

TINA CHANG

MANKIND IS SO FALLIBLE

after Heather Altfeld

We lay down to the day as if we could flee
from the body's burden. On the ground are notes,
candles, a saint's face painted alive with gold.

Where does God live if not in the shadows
of struggle, marching next to the living,
with battlements and a slogan, knowing

faintly more than we do? Someone dispatches
a call for help. Someone notes the patches
on a man's jacket. Somewhere there is a circle

of people praying and dying at once, the loss
of which makes a narrative rain down
in news feeds across frames of light.

*

My mother once gave up her savior,
walked into our living room to profess
her love for the here and now.

She no longer believed in the unseen,
could no longer bow to invisible idols.
She sat on the chair in front of me

more mortal than she ever was,
face lit with resolve, done with faith,
done with the promise of rapture.

Somewhere, glass breaks
and the one who damages
wears a mask of God's many faces.

Tina Chang

*

How would the body be summoned
if we started over? Imagine a blank book
in which the body is drawn.

Would the body lie horizontal like a violin
whose music plays off key or would it stand
upright like a totem pole against its own weather?

I place a book under my pillow
as the ancient Japanese courtesans did
to dream the body into being.

Wind gathers from the past until I am walking
in snow. The arms and legs move in unison
with the mind, an engine of sinew and meat.

How should I draw it, not the body
but what it contains. Not its contours
but its tensions. Not its stew of blood

and clattering bones but its promise.
I prefer now to think of the body's debt
and what is owes to the ledger of the living.

*

I imagine the courtesans rising from sleep,
hair rushing to the waist like ink. They rub
their eyes of dream, tighten their robes

as they lift the book from beneath their pillow
as if urging a stone from its bedrock.
How would they think of the body then,

having wakened from that place

one could describe as near death.
Instead, the body startles forward toward infinity.

*

The courtesan runs her hand along the page,
feels the blank space, an urgent bell summons her.
Dips her brush in ink and runs it along an emptiness.

When a young man enters a church,
he seeks a furnace to burn away his hatred
and a foundation on which to kneel.

He seeks his mother's mercy
and his father's vengeance. He passes through
the doors and we call this worship.

If it could be as simple as sleep, curling inward
toward an avalanche of hummingbirds, the mind
frees itself as the body lets go its earthly wreckage.

If it could be like enduring the wholeness of a dream
so real we dissolve into a veil of the past,
wind dragged backward, brutal in its disappearance.

JENNIFER KWON DOBBS

ELEGY FOR A SONG BETWEEN

Kim Sang Pil / Phillip Clay (1974–2017)

I didn't know you, so I cradle the sound
between Phillip / Sang Pil—*friend*

of horses, fortune writing. A song between
Phil / Pil swayed a brass bell

chime inside your heart's chamber. I'm guessing
a wild stampede, the gray ghost

ripple of their dappled muscles. You
brave and alone offered stolen bicycles

to their power wounding the ground.
Whatever stood between them

their hooves pummeled
back to a root web. No—that's glib

for the unknown handiwork that scarred
my older brother before orphaning him

to the angels' ledgers. The math that took him
renamed him. The math that removed him

renamed him again. No citizen. Illegible
the angels coveted paper: "He used all of our ink

to print his weird books," Holt's daughter said
at his funeral, as birth files faded

locked in moving bookcases. (Joan, you tried
decades to retrieve yours.) How many

pills did I steal then swallow as your sister
trapped in Oklahoma? Who knows

the flowers' names the Koreans prefer
to blanket heaven's threshold?

PREETI KAUR RAJPAL

DIRGE AFTER OAK CREEK

but before charleston. somewhere between.

america:
enter

the gurdwara door is open
our bare feet like cracked glass
our covered heads bulletproof from ego
we turn our backs on bellingham
build our gurdwaras from post traumatic cinder
of bombed birmingham black church
nina simone sings
tera bhaana meetha laage
may your will taste sweet to me
to tune of mississippi goddamn
gunpowder lines noses of children who ran
women who hid in the langar kitchen closet
holy men who sing praise and wind

the fbi publishes   a white paper
he acted alone   of course

the love that forgives a lullaby
which sears obedient
into a bittering lemon

TARFIA FAIZULLAH

READING CELAN AT THE LIBERATION WAR MUSEUM

Independence Day Celebration 2011, Dhaka

i.

In a courtyard, in these stacks of chairs
        before the empty stage—*near are*
we Lord, near and graspable. Lord,
        accept these humble offerings:

stacks of biscuits wrapped in cellophane,
        stacks of bone in glass: thighbone,
spine. Stacks of white saucers, porcelain
        circles into which stacks of lip-worn

cups slide neat. Jawbone, Lord. Galleries
        of laminated clippings declaring war.
Hands unstack chairs into rows. *The dead:*
        they still go begging. What for, Lord?

Blunt bayonets, once sharp as wind?
        Moon-pale stacks of clavicle? A hand—

ii.

Moon-pale stacks of clavicle a hand
        brushes dust from. *I lost a word*

that was left to me: sister. The wind
        severs through us—we sit, wait

for songs of nation and loss in neat
        long rows below this leaf-green

flag—its red-stitched circle stains
      us blood-bright blossom, stains

us river-silk—*I saw you, sister, standing*
      in this brilliance—I saw light sawing

through a broken car window, thistling
      us pink—I saw, sister, your bleeding

head, an unfurling shapla flower
      petaling slow across mute water—

    iii.

Petaling slow
      across mute water,
bows of trawlers
       skimming nets
of silver fish that ripple
       through open
hands that will carve them
        skin-
less. *We were hands,*
      we scooped
the darkness empty. We
       are rooted
bodies in rows silent before
       the sparked
blue limbs of dancers
      leafing the dark
light indigo, then
     jasmine alighting
into a cup, then
     hands overturning
postcards bearing flag
      and flower, hands
cradling the replica of a boat,

hands

thrust there and into

nothingness. You,

a corpse, sister, bathed

jasmine, blue—

iv.

A corpse: sister, bathed jasmine. Blue,

the light leading me from this gift shop

into

a gallery of gray stones: *Heartgray puddles,*
two mouthfuls of silence: the shadow

cast by the portrait of a raped woman trapped

in a frame, face hidden behind her own black

river of hair: photo that a solemn girl

your corpse's age stands still and small

before. She asks, *Did someone hurt her?*

Did she do something bad? Her mother

does not reply. Her father turns,

shudders,

as the light drinks our silences, parched—

as I too turn in light, spine-scraped—

you teach you teach your hands to sleep

v.

you teach you teach your hands to sleep

because her hands can't hold the shape

of a shapla flower cut from its green leaf

because her hands can't hold grief

nor light nor sister   in her hands fistfuls

of her own hair   on her wrists glass bangles

like the one you struggled over your hand

the same hand that slapped a sister's wan

face   look   the young girl stands before

the photo of the young woman who swore

she would not become the old woman

crouched low on a jute mat holding

out to you a bangle   *a strange lostness was*

bodily present   you came near to living

vi.

Bodily present, you came near to living,
        Poet, in this small blue dress still stained,

the placard states, with the blood of the child
        crushed dead by a soldier's boot. Who failed

and fails?—nights you couldn't bear the threshed
        sounds of your heart's hard beating. I press

a button: 1971 springs forth: black and white
        bodies marching in pixelated rows. Nights

you resuscitated *the Word, sea-overflowed,*
        star-overflown. A pixelated woman tied

with a white rope to a black pole, her white
        sari embroidered with mud or blood. Nights

you were the *wax to seal what's unwritten—*
        the screen goes white in downdrifting light.

      vii.

The screen goes white. In downdrifting light,
        the stairwell is a charred tunnel. We walk out
of it into the couttyard—my skirt flares a rent
        into the burnt evening. *Something was silent,*

something went its way—something gnashes
        inside me, sister—along the yellow gashes
of paint guiding me through these rooms lined
        with glass cases, past machine gun chains

shaped into the word *Bangla.* Here, on this
        stage, a dancer bows low her limbs
once more before us. The stage goes silent.
        We gather ourselves: souvenirs of bone.

Pray, Lord. We are near. Near are we, Lord—

Tarfia Faizullah

in a courtyard, in these stacks of chairs.

SHIN YU PAI

BURNING MONK

From the remains
of his cremation,
the monks recovered

the seat of Thich Quang Duc's
consciousness—

a bloodless protest
to awaken the heart
of the oppressor

offered
at the crossing of
Phanh Dinh Phung
   & Le Van Duyet
doused in gasoline &
immolated by 4-meter
flames the orange-robed

arhat folded in
the stillness
of full lotus

his body withering
his crown blackening
his flesh charring
his corpse collapsing

his heart refusing to burn
his heart refusing to burn
his heart refusing to burn

SHIN YU PAI

EASTER SUNDAY

This morning my husband shaves
the lawn, the grass trimmer

choking up before the yard
is fully manicured,

we keep our shoes on
at our neighbor's flat

Maundy & Paschal greetings—
traditions we leave behind
in Anatole

at the host's table someone
counts the number of skeptics
out at sunrise

clipping the green while
overheard from
the kitchen

I decided to give up
Lent for Lent

not one
to be outdone
the native scribbler shows

off her sculpting chops
in yellow marshmallow
tableaux, the memoir of

her characters retold
through sugar-spun rabbits,

a gelatin hostess gift

for the vegetarian mistress
of the household, indelible
while tomorrow

marks the start of
Rwandan Genocide Memorial
Week, remembering

eight days into April
the poet of Boston's Joy Street

who imagined a new
cross in the wind
a communion

where we are
altered by another's
charity, taken aback

by the soft
push of breath
against a cheek

FAISAL MOHYUDDIN

IN DEFENSE OF MONSTERS

"What the image does not show is that I had talked to other witnesses to try and find out what was happening, to see if I could be of any help, even though enough people were at the scene tending to the victims. I then decided to call my family to say that I was fine and was making my way home from work, assisting a lady along the way by helping her get to Waterloo station. My thoughts go out to all the victims and their families. I would like to thank Jamie Lorriman, the photographer who took the picture, for speaking to the media in my defence."

–The Muslim woman on Westminster Bridge, London, March 22, 2017

Let them monster the world's Muslims, monster our pain
by saying we pay no mind, monster our living hurt

with the phantom aches they've fabricated in factories that once,
in some dream, produced goods good enough to rival

God's own work. Let them monster their invented heartache,
grafting it onto the living hurts that their own kind rubbled

into their lives, leaving them so broken their eyes had nowhere safe
to turn except onto our faces whose incandescent beauty

filled them with such massive libraries of shame they needed
again the native strength of our shoulders to carry

their brittle bodies into others' regions of panic. They'll conquer
and concoct new names for these lands, too, thieving

with one invented victory after another any claim we hold

to goodness. Let them monster us and those who survived before us

and continue to survive the monstering, be it as living things
on a bridge beneath the gaze of Big Ben, in mosques

in Canada and America and Pakistan and Yemen and Iran
and Palestine and Myanmar and Germany and China

where our blood on the sidewalk, the wall, the window, the front
page of the newspaper, the back page of policy, is our burden

to wash. And so on and so forth on battered battlegrounds
where our own bodies have been blown to bits by the monsters

who claim our names and turn to the monstering ones
and say, Raise us up as your saviors, and make us your healing

flames. Let them be saved by such imposters whose bloody crimes
nourish their monstering minds, guide their monstering hands

as they sculpt, from the thin air of worry, towers of fear,
rejection, exclusion, law, and more and more cries for war,

for bombs, for the absolute annihilation of us. Let them monster
their own monstering, monster their own laundered history,

trading one monster for another, surrendering once again,
but this time with flailing arms and drowning soul,

to the monsters in their blood. Let them monster any explosive word
we might utter in protest, or in compassion, or in self-

healing, until it's a silenced angel, for—don't you understand yet?—
when they've already monstered us beyond recognition,

we might as well just swallow the pain of being monstered,
help some old lady cross the street, away from the destruction,

do that instead of fighting back, then plunge into the obliterating
rush of the subway. What better way to let them monster

their own destinies and the promised greatness of their oversold
tomorrows. Let them be free to monster every great nation

that promises better, monster the goodness of these lands,
monster the earth living beyond the flay of their shortsightedness,

monster God Himself until what's left is nothing but
the monstering darkness of their own cries, cutting through

the cruel echoes of their dying breaths, their final pleas for tolerance,
or something like that, reverberating through the silence.

BARBARA JANE REYES

IN THE CITY, A NEW CONGREGATION FINDS HER

She keeps safe our memory when nothing's committed to stone.
Sibilant selvedge woman, thread and knots talkstory woman.

She whose memories not paperbound, lover of midnight words.
Scrawled myth upon flesh woman, indigo testimony tattoo woman.

We bring her spirits we've captured in bottles.
Fire water woman, imbibes the spirits woman.

We bring her dried tobacco leaves and tea.
Exhales the word woman, fullmoon weaving woman.

She looses her thick hair from its pins and coils.
Litany liturgy woman, stitching suture woman.

She settles into her favorite chair, she always begins like this.
Soul gatherer woman, spiderweb songbird woman.

She breathes steam from tea, steeped stems and petals.
Piece and patchwork woman, down home cookin' woman.

She crushes anise stars, sweetens nightmare into reverie.
Stone by stone woman, singed and soot woman.

She cups glazed clay between cracked hands.
Silver winged bird woman, riverine dream-filled woman.

She rubs together palms callused, she who conjures for us a feast.
Sugar tinctured moonwoman, twittering songstress moonwoman.

She whose eyes widen with black thundercloud and sea.
Salt luster sirenwoman, winter solstice madwoman.

She whose voice billows and peals, she whose eyes gaze nowhere.

Barbara Jane Reyes

Howling nomad madwoman, cut the bullshit madwoman.

Her lips release language not of paper sometimes (we think) she forgets.
Older than the ocean woman, sargassum and seashell woman.

She who has kept vigil always, she of the wing-kissed sunset.
Sipping starlight woman, before there was a nailed god woman.

BARBARA JANE REYES

THE GOSPEL OF JUANA DE LA CRUZ

in the beginning with the word, there was
your breakfast, your bed, your benefits package
a woman sent, whose name was Juana
your myths, your medicine, your maid for hire

all things were made by her; and without her
your leisure and pleasure, your cheap labor pool
was not any thing made that was made
your tech, your toys, your purchasing power

inside her, all life, and the life of man
your love, your lunch, your urban renewal
she overcame darkness, she came to bear
your realm, your retail, your dollars at work

she came to give testimony, she was the word
your trinkets, your tongue, your taste for travel
and from her fullness you have all received
your savior, your supper, and always, your succor—

ADEEBA SHAHID TALUKDER

ON BEAUTY

When I was 19, I trembled
to meet men's eyes.

Scarf, *burqa*, black
eyeliner. I was more
than Muslim,
more than beautiful,
more than sexual.

They wanted to know
what they could not
see.

    *

The cruel beloved of Urdu
poetry slays her lovers

with glances, leaving them
to sigh and wither, and in this

intricacy is power:

I cannot lift
a suitcase, which means
I will never have to.

    *

James once wrote me
stories and poems as Majnoon,
as the nightingale, as the prey.

He said he could pretend

to be Muslim,

as long as you know you're the only god
I'll ever worship.

*

We cannot exist for long
at high energy levels.
Something, somewhere,
will collapse.

The beloved must remain

cruel, or this collapse
is all the more inevitable.

*

You're crazy, I'd say.
Not crazy. He would reply. *Mad.*
Mad—say, as a moth.

(He had read my poems.)

Like Patty Boyd,
I became Laila. I wrote
back. It lasted, perhaps,

a month.

*

You see, these were not his stories,
or Eric Clapton's.
He did not know the
meaning of *fanaa*. He could not.

*

Perhaps there is no
such thing as the evil eye,
or such a thing as God
in love.

Why, then, do the children
throw stones at Majnoon,
at the swan in Glencoe Lake?

How is it that I cannot see a trace
of beauty in the clear water?

*

As the lake thaws and the winds
grow gentler, there is nothing in the air
to reach out and touch.

If I hadn't told him, during an episode:
You are my everything—

if I hadn't told him:
you'll never understand, you're white—

would he orbit me still?

PURVI SHAH

BEATING HER SOILED CLOTHES, SARASWATI REACHES GOD AND BURSTS INTO TEARS

"In Hinduism the first menstruation of a young girl is a cause for celebration, with special presents given. However menstrual blood has generally been considered impure. At my grandmother's house, women were not permitted to cook in the kitchen, had different utensils, ate and slept separately. They were also not allowed to enter the prayer room. Nonetheless, when as a 12-year-old girl I visited my grandparents during the summer holidays, my loving and pragmatic grandmother spared me this embarrassment by asking me to not tell anyone about my periods!"

—**Kumkum Bhatia, "Why can't girls enter temples during menstruation?"**, *South Asian Parent*

Where the river pulls off red

         veil or living

shroud, a tiger sparks

Purvi Shah

in woman's breast. When no one

is watching, the tiger learns

to swim. It follows the river   as river makes

as if there were no day nor night, no moons to keep mark. The river has nowhere

to be, no one to carry, no fabric to fold, no births to assume, no opinion to praise, no red

blotches to whiten, no sleep to solitaire, nowhere to hide sore breasts, no need to compete

the black cloud

for lavish rains, nowhere

always going — absorbing

to go as it is always going there — there

curd of sea, absorbing salts off a girl's thigh, blood

off a woman's smile.   Forgive your smeared

compound, lair

for your cramp

scrap, piles for

everything that is

usable, this stack

of your own

future limbs. You want

the power to turn

Purvi Shah

a trident into a spoon, your hand

as the first cup from which a toddler

drinks.   You

                believe

                                        you can

                talk to river, calm it down, reason it. *Woman,*

have you not   *learned?*

You may birth   your ruler.

You feel every

contamination.

These waters,

clumped fabrics

feet.

destination but perfection in this lifetime, your sore

skin as moon origin, as bountiful

At river's gather —

Measure: 21 feet. Measure: 27

of you.

scar

how they bear

rings, tried

wombs, incarnations

Purvi Shah

After encountering

as only water can — moving without

tiger, I spun my destiny

moving, being without breaking

whole. My lifetimes

are prowling

that could never be

seen.

Purvi Shah

too.

tiding

conceived. Women rip

around me, keening longings,

hopes. Mark

come apart,

come home.

were river

since this river

these spilled wants

the streaks of my salvation:

Mark the blood of my limbs: once they

KENJI C. LIU

MIGRATORY DAUGHTER

You've recycled your life,
    quit this ragged field
        leaving papers and
            bones of language.
Undocumented
    bodhisattva,
        penumbra scattered
        around us.
Citizen ship unswayed
    by the thirsty republic,
        no postal address
            for the waxing moon.
Your letters bear kanji
    neat in /na ni nu ne/
        so no dreams
            in English ka?
All your choices
    have followed you
        into the next.
            So will mine.
Everyone is broken.
    Band-aids. Cedar and sage,
        hot apple cider,
            sharp rush of Tiger Balm.
People hurry forward
    as if unanimous,
        part the incoming tide
        with oiled noses.
Forget dust. We are mostly water
    and so is the Earth.
        Ashes to ashes.
            Water to generous water.

SARAH GAMBITO

VIRGINIA

We were brown and immigrant. We drove a Volkswagen and
sang songs in the hymnals of white people. We loved these songs.
And god was pinned to the underside of my skirt like a blood
orchid.

I loved a boy named Philip. My mother sent me to his house with
100 eggrolls that she fried herself. We kissed until my tongue was
tired. I didn't know that— that the tongue could get tired, like
any muscle.

I wore my own clothes on Halloween. I smudged my eyes with
eyeliner and dotted my neck with two black dots.

What are you?

A victim.

I flapped my arms like a pinwheel. Solar winds flooded me. I
didn't dare to think I could not belong. I was a wrapped baby of
a kind of oriole. Wiping the sun's juice off my face, I balanced on
a pencil drawing of health insurance.

I wanted to be a poem. Ox-like, my family rose against me.
Incensed, I could think of nothing else. Love abounding
Loveabounding. If my family met a poem, they would really
punch her in the face.

Huddled around the one bulb of health insurance, I said I
wanted to be a poem. The poem played piano. Her arm muscles
moved and she opened her voice and I knew she loved her
husband, her children, her dog, her country. In this song, I saw
the chips of mica in the asphalt. I held the cans of super saver. I
touched bankruptcy and rusted bike chains. The tiny dot of my
sister on the palomino of school leaving and then coming back

again and then leaving, ad infinitum.

I had a brass portrait of the Pietà. Her lambent and impassive face looking down on the broken body, the broken language. The deep kelp of not belonging. Together we watched the tide go in and out of the fresh sown batteries of our country.

A draft of this poem would be good to read/to send to you.

K-MING CHANG

REINCARNATION

I.

in my first life, I married a soldier
        with my father's hands, the same ring
        finger curling into a trigger, the same dull
dogtags around his neck, blank

of names. my husband prefers me clean
        shaven, blanked between the legs.
        in nanking, women saved themselves
by burying their bodies alive. I imagine

they are still alive, underground
        in a city of women, unraised. I was raised
        by my mother's fist, softened
to earth beneath her knuckles. she beat out

my shape from river clay, silt & soiled
        sheets. every lesson was the same: *do*
        not fear death
        in this country
you have never truly

been alive. in this country,
        I am tired
        of seeing the same death
in different bodies. I am tired

of my husband emptying himself
        like a barrel, our backyard
        gaped into a pit, bones bleaching
the soil white. ghosts

knocking out

our doors like teeth.

I.

in my first life, I was never
    born. I floated inside
    my mother like the dead
sea.

or,

in my first life, I was born
    exactly on time, my father
    tying the umbilical cord
into a noose, an exchange:

his life for mine. my life for
    -getting what it owes. I kiss
    a girl with the only mouth
I own, ask to be for

-given to her hands, I burn
    fast as a field. I want
    to be touched everywhere
like a season.

I want the heart to swing
    in its cage, ringing each rib
    like a windchime. Her breath
the wind. Her scent

like something trampled
    into grass. I fit my fist
    into the soil, snug as a seed.
I watch it grow a corpse

of trees, an orchard so full
    it falls on its knees. I fall

to my knees, shut the space
between us like a door.

The room shrinks to fit our bodies
   exactly. I wet my tongue
   on her skin & she crosses
my body in one lick.

We touch with whole oceans
   our fingertips.

CRAIG SANTOS PEREZ

THE PATRON SAINT OF BINGO

for grandma perez (1922–2018)

Bingo is not indigenous
to Guam, yet here we are
in the air-conditioned
community center next to
the village Catholic church.

You set the bingo cards
and ink daubers on the table.
You sit in your wheelchair
like an ancient sea turtle.

This is your daily ritual, daily
prayer. The last time I played
bingo with you was 25 years
ago, when I was still a teenager
and still lived on-island. I

remember when you won,
you never shouted "bingo"
too boastfully. When you lost,
you merely said, "Agupa',
tomorrow, we'll feel lucky."

Either way, you always smiled
during bingo. Here, no one
punishes you for speaking
Chamorro. Here, no war
invades and occupies life.
Here, no soldiers force you
to bow to a distant emperor,
or pledge allegiance to a violent
flag. Here, no nation steals

our land. Here, you're safe
To gossip and play.

You watch the bingo balls turn
in the wire cage like giant beads
from a broken rosary. You turned
95 years old this year, making you
the eldest manåmko' in this room.

I no longer attend mass, yet
here I am praying to the patron
saint of bingo to call forth
your fateful combination
of letters and numbers.

I pray for you to win
not for the gambler's rush
or the sin of money. I pray
for you to win because
you carry so much loss,
having outlived grandpa
and most of your childhood
friends. Suddenly, someone

shouts, "Bingo!" You sigh,
put down the ink dauber,
and sink back into the shell
of your wheelchair.

"When's your flight," you ask.
"Agupa', grandma. Tomorrow."
But today I feel so lucky
for this chance to play bingo
with you one last time.

SHANKAR NARAYAN

INVOCATION FOR THE IMPOSSIBLE PRESENT

Let me be
unseen. Let me outwit the eyes
of this cycle. Watch Indiana Jones eat chilled monkey

brain. By existing
I am threat. By existing as human
I am prayer. I want only to be

a flyover state. I want only a pebble
as my emblem. Let me be crushed
into infinitesimal voids in the infinity

of the sandbox. Let Mojo destroy
the Powerpuff Girls. Insert the opener into my eye
and press play. Rotating like the Exorcist I will centrifuge

all my demons. I'm forgetting
all my devotions. But at least I have an open
mind. Let me be

beautiful cyborg. I don't need to be
all-powerful, just to feel colors and earthquakes
in ways no human has. Make possible my plea, quiet

sometimes or algorithmic as a tsunami breaking over a single human
standing on an endless Normandy of grey
silicon. Watch the wave grow into the creature

from the black lagoon. I'm finally remembering
your existence. My ecstasy loops light up. Let us be
so entangled. If you jump let me jump with you. Our crowns are off, brains open

for business—sprinkle chips like peanut butter cups in Disneyland
soft serve. Remake me
Nebraska. Let Om Puri kill Indiana. Remembering your body

gets harder over time. Retention schedules and such. Let the wave's
soldering and circuitry render me moot. Let's ride it
together like a mother-

board, let it be green and grey like your precisely two eyes

the last time we made love with angel bodies levitating
all around us, the eight breathless propellers

of our entanglement, googling us through Swarovski crystals
split four ways like fisheyes that never leave the water's
surface. Rend me open, let your gorgons stare

into my turmoil. Because all my base are belong
to you. Just give me back the right to be
forgotten. Anything is possible in this universe

except my body.

JOSEPH O. LEGASPI

EASTER, BONIFACIO HIGH STREET

*a "mixed-use development"—huge shopping mall—in Bonifacio
Global City, Metro Manila*

Between the Coffee Bean & Tea Leaf and The Body Shop
a station of the Cross. On a trodden lawn browning into
desert, two lines are formed for shoppers to be Christ-like.
Christ-lite, puns the Pinoy. The devout come forward to suffer,
put their suffering on display. They'd strap a stretch of varnished
four-by-four across their shoulders, ropes tied around their wingspan
arms, the weight of sins redeemed by Jesus on his march to Calvary.
Assisted by the fine volunteers of the Church of Christ wearing
designer t-shirts, the aspiring saviors lumber towards salvation.
As with a slender petite woman handing over her Coach
purse to her surly boyfriend while she is yoked like a carabao,
the Philippine national animal of heroic industrious tolerance.
The carriers circle each other around the astro turf like sushi
on a conveyor belt. And nearby down the square, a full cross
is offered. Ideal for groups, its holy length delivers camaraderie.
Friends, family, frenemies lift in harmony, wholesale redemption.
They pause, pose for pictures, their selfie sticks a mirroring sky.
To reenact is to worship in the highest form: Jesus stumbled,
his sinners lifted him up. Witness an elder harness the giant
cross at its crossing while a child carries the tail end. At the crown
a tall youth can't part with his shopping bag, so on both shoulders he
slings, the Abercrombie & Fitch models brandishing their pectorals, godly.

LI-YOUNG LEE

CUCKOO FLOWER ON THE WITNESS STAND

I sang in a church choir during one war
American TV made famous.

I fled a burning archipelago in the rain,
on my mother's back, in another war
nobody televised.

In the midst of wars worldwide, many
in places whose names I can't pronounce,
my father taught me, "When asked
about your knowledge of politics, answer, 'None.'"

I doodled in the church bulletin on Sundays
while my father offered the twenty-minute Pastor's Prayer.

Every morning, I tucked Adam's promise and Jesus' disgrace
together with my pajamas under my pillow,
unable to distinguish which of them
was God's first thought, and which God's second.

When asked about my religious training, I answer,
"I seek my destiny in my origin."

Most of my life, I've answered politely
to questions put to me, speaking only when spoken to,

a sign of weakness
unbefitting of any free human being.

Therefore, for the sake of free human beings everywhere,
and because no one asked, I now say:

My voice's taper graduates to smoke,

dividing every word between us,
what was meant and what was heard.

And speech's bird
threads hunger's needle
or perishes in a thicket of words.

And so, speaking as one of the flowers,
I'll seek rest in falling.

I'll seek asylum in the final word,
an exile from the first word,
and refugee of an illegible past.

DEAREST FATHER, FORGIVE ME FOR I HAVE SEEN:
ON DOUBT AND QUESTIONS OF FAITH

OCEAN VUONG

PRAYER FOR THE NEWLY DAMNED

Dearest Father, forgive me for I have seen.
Behind the wooden fence, a field lit
with summer, a man pressing a shank
to another man's throat. Steel turning to light
on sweat-slick neck. Forgive me
for not twisting this tongue into the shape
of Your name. For thinking:
this must be how every prayer
begins—the word *Please* cleaving
the wind into fragments, into what
a boy hears in his need to know
how pain blesses the body back
to its sinner. The hour suddenly
stilled. The man, his lips pressed
to the black boot. Am I wrong to love
those eyes, to see something so clear
& blue—beg to remain clear
& blue? Did my cheek twitch
when the wet shadow bloomed from his crotch
& trickled into ochre dirt? How quickly
the blade becomes You. But let me begin
again: There's a boy kneeling
in a house with every door kicked open
to summer. There's a question corroding
his tongue. A knife touching
Your finger lodged inside the throat.
Dearest Father, what becomes of the boy
no longer a boy? *Please*—
what becomes of the shepherd
when the sheep are cannibals?

MATTHEW OLZMANN

NATE BROWN IS LOOKING FOR A MOOSE

Shrouded in fog, dignified and reticent: a moose.
When Ross White goes outside in Vermont,
he sees one immediately.

When Jamaal May goes outside, he sees one as well.
As if they are everywhere.

But when Nate Brown goes outside, he sees
only the absence of a moose, spaces
where one might have stood but no longer stands.

He's been hoping to see one for years.
So he practices his moose call and nothing happens.
He stands tiptoe, on one leg,
narrows his eyes. Nothing happens.

What he has now is a mission, a quest
a calling that can't be denied.

It's dusk and he stares into the dark. The world
is full of dogwoods and elm trees, and behind the branches,
ten thousand more—all leafy and stupid
and yielding no answers.

What do I mean? I mean
despite everything, we might search
for something and never find it.

When I was a teenager, several of my friends
suddenly found God.
I tried, but found only pocket lint and angst.

The loser of some holy scavenger hunt,
the last to cross the finish line,

kneeling in church, whispering
to heaven: *Dude, where are you?*

What made it worse was everyone's conviction.
The candles and prayer groups,
the smugness of their repeating, *Well, you know,*
if you look behind you and see only one set of footprints—

What makes Nate Brown's quest equally difficult
is how our friend Chip Cheek leans back in his chair
and says, *Oh Man—out here they grow big as dinosaurs.*

And how Kellam Ayers's eyes fill with mist
when she nods and says, *Yes, they're almost   magical.*

And so a man goes back into the fields
and tries not to move. Goes
out to the forest and tries not to move. Goes
down to the river
and pretends he's part of that river.

He is a stone, a branch, a fallen maple leaf.
He is (sort of) patient
and he'll see this thing or hold his breath forever.

I think of myself as a teenager and how
I'm no different now.

At home, my wife has a numbness, a weakness that spreads
through her body and no doctors
can figure it out. When she sleeps,

I'm afraid of everything and I pray into her hair
like I'm young again
on my knees in a church, in search of an answer.

Sometimes I go outside and the dark is so prodigious—
the way it remedies everything by covering everything.

Matthew Olzmann

I like thinking of how my friend stares
down this same darkness
as if it will offer the index to some temporal secret.

What we're looking for are miracles.

Out there—
there could be nothing.

Or there could be antlers and hooves.
Lumbering mysteries.
They plod across the quiet fields.

VIKAS MENON

SAMADHI

Fuck silence. I want
to hear what Buddha heard

at enlightenment: was it
the sneer of air escaping

the hatch? The crinkling
of paper as humankind danced,

cut-out silhouettes, amuse-
bouches for the Gods?

Did all questions still?
Or was it a cacophony—

a thousand wrong answers
spoken at once?

Or was it just

his breath,
in and out,

light seeping
through his eyelids,

the hush of a sparrow,

the wet warmth
of its droppings,

the tremble of an ant
clinging to a branch,

the gentle murmur of leaf & lung,

their eversprung, sweet-fisted
pumping.

KAZIM ALI

COVER ME

Such clamorwaves guide old vision's whisper

Voice against whose virtue another version crashes

Mosques vanish back to ocean ocean vanish back to vision

Vision elide the remembrance of what is it we remember

Could you say this moment rubs the slate blank

When what rises up from the basket after you denied yourself

On the far shore I am still trying to spit out

What they mean they mean after all the trees and statues have
    fallen

Wing cave acrobatic as if we weren't already told a million
    different times

Weave no future together or on a different day the sun

Boiling in my pocket and such haunting will splinter the rib

From its cage and you will have to admit

It has pleased you   it has relieved you

It has made you remember   you always wanted this

The feeling of fruit torn from the tree

What you wouldn't give to be miragined like that

What wouldn't you have given to be forgiven

To be forgotten then missed then sought for and found

Cover me cover me

Grief godmine what hasn't changed has changed

HYEJUNG KOOK

INVENTION NO. 9 IN F MINOR

for two voices

A pang, spangled, fire fangled—
How often the little stab

the golden spear poised lightly
shakes me. *How terribly I want*

in his hand as she swoons, head thrown back,
what is not mine, what others have,

openmouthed, pain and sweetness carrying her
what may yet come to me,

out of herself,
I'd burn ox bones wrapped

rapt bride of God.
in the bloodied lace

Marble made flesh made spirit.
of caul fat, flinching but persistent

Dear Teresa,
when sizzle struck me, seared me

when you wore a hair shirt, tied nettles to your wrists,
marked me. I'd sit zazen for days,

⌠   used olive twigs to throw up
⌡ *left hand cupping the right,*

⌠   to ensure you could receive the Host,
⌡ *holding empty egg-shaped air.*

⌠ how did you contain
⌡ *If I thought it would fulfill*

⌠ yourself, find such joy
⌡   *this want, grant me*

⌠ in the bridling   of desire?
⌡   *the little birdling of my desire.*

MICHELLE PEÑALOZA

VESTIGE

The creak of pews makes my knees ache,
my palms and fingertips kiss.
Phosphorus, censers, old mahogany,
boxed wine, candle wax
work upon me like the itches
of an old collared jumper.
Worship seeps from memory to body.
I confess to the air.
Forgive me, Air, I cannot believe.
It has been three years since my last quiet.
I hold a rosary, count its beads
like the redolent string of rose petals
my Lola held close when she died.
After prayer, the attar melded with the garlic
bouquet of her hands, bulbous
scents cradling, caressing my face.
I roll each pressed round between
my forefinger and thumb, keep count:
my guilt, my guilt, my doubt—
I am not free. I cup the tangled strand,
pass it between my hands. The attar
now lives in the leaf creases of my palms.
The quiet whispers, *scent is memory's companion.*
I inhale calla lilies, yeast of Eucharist,
and my mother's undulating voice
wailing the Rosary at my Lola's funeral.
My mother looked like artwork then,
something of Bernini's—her ecstasy carved
into relief by her pain.
I remember cathedral light washed her face.
I envied the faith she found, her ravished heart.
Once, an old man spoke to me of faith
in dishes. How he held, washed, and dried
each dish as though it were a child in his sink—
the dishes themselves, and the fact that I am here
washing them, are miracles. I count the day's
miracles: the sweet butter on wheat toast,

the abundance of coffee, the predictability of doors,
opening and closing. The stars held within an apple,
the sound of eight separate rivers
converged in one spot, working in one measure.
Rosaries and rose petals and garlic.
Vinegar and incense and wine.

SHIREEN MADON

RELIGION

There were ghosts in the garden
when we were young, obvious as suns.

Our shuttered, too-American home
choked with rhododendron.

We were careful to navigate
inconvenient stories like land mines.

Stashed sticks of sandalwood
in drawers with framed prophets.

When Grandma came, she unpacked
talcum powder to whiten her skin

and told me to stop exercising
or I'd end up with muscles like a man.

When I stopped praying one summer,
my father lost his tongue in grief.

That year, we strung the pine
with silences. Brush fires sputtered

pathetically like crates of bodega pomegranates.
That's to say, we loved more poorly.

When Grandma died, like an exodus
we emptied of language and gifts of gold.

We sold a little of our identity each day
until our bones were bleached of histories

and gurus that had kept us safe. All we can
hope is to be bodied again.

CHRISTIAN DETISCH

CONVERSION

I do not know the source that brings us light.
           Think Paul. Think conversion,
      with the fervor and emptiness
of some white-hot vat of liquid steel...

We do not all fall upon such strokes
           of instant, shocking fright that leave us
      so complete; yet I praise the wholeness
of some lonely thing, the woman at her porch

who slowly drags her cigarette, and feels
           the final, fleeting bite of embers
      die upon her feet. My grief
resists such unfamiliar touch—it's grace

compelling us toward what we don't know.
           O unwilled electric surge of spine,
      of mind, of force beyond all my now-known reckoning,
make me lie down. Teach me to be small.

VANDANA KHANNA

BLUE MADONNA

Back before color threaded
the world, when everything
was in black-and-white, I was
the only pagan at school, hiding
my breath with its curry and accent,
mouthing words to prayers I didn't
understand. I wondered why there
were always holy men but no holy
women. I wanted to be enchanted,
to steal the baby Jesus from the Christmas
play and keep him hidden in my closet,
pull him out when I needed to be saved.
I wanted to be the blue Madonna holding
all the pieces of her son together.

Half a world away, girls my age came
as close to God as anyone could be.
They were already throwing their bodies
over their husband's funeral pyres, flung
out like blankets over the flames, chanting
Ram, Ram like a nursery rhyme. My mother
told me it was a holy mantra, the more I said
it, the holier I would be, but I never really knew
how or why, just that it was supposed to happen.
Once I tried saying it as many times as I could
in fifty seconds, but nothing. No miracle,
no halo of thorns around my head. And all I
could think about were those girls, widows
at fifteen. What did burning flowers smell like?
Something terrible, something holy?

W. TODD KANEKO

ATHEISM

And because there are no angels
ascending in order, it's easy

to leave everything to chance.
There are no demons, either—

just mosquitos that flit around
porch lights, near screen doors.

The insects don't confuse the soul
with our system of arteries

and hearts criss-crossing
this scaly planet. We are hairy

knuckles and sharp teeth
and we savagely make love

like it will make us holy.
When there is a buzzing

in our ears, it's easy to swat
at the bloodsuckers and go back

to gnawing on the bones.
Out in the backyard, the angels

gather near the bug zapper
and dissipate into lightning.

TIMOTHY LIU

LOVE POEM IN A STEAM ROOM RUN BY SUFIS

Hard to commit
to memory—their knees

brushing up against

my own as we recited
lines no one knew

by heart—our nostrils

singed—burnt scent
of eucalyptus as we got on

with the business

at hand not to be found
in any book of verse.

FELIZ LUCIA MOLINA

HELLO KITTY VIRGIN MARY

For as long as I've known her, my mother's two things are going to Mass at Our Lady of Peace and playing bingo in North Hollywood. Guilty from leaving me at home all night, she'd bring a pink paper bag with Sanrio characters printed all over it. Every week would be different inside. The size of the bag would depend on if she got lucky that night or if she broke even, which she believed was the same as winning. Inside, there were stickers, pencils, a pencil case, paper, lollipops, a diary. It was the period when Pochacco just came out and I was skeptical of transitioning out of my love for Hello Kitty and onto smaller more obscure colorful characters. My mother knew this because she could read my mind, so she only bought Hello Kitty things.

I would stay up until midnight and wait for when she'd pull up in her white Cadillac onto the concrete driveway. Smelling like Marlboro Reds which I associated with evil, she'd wake me up from being somewhere between half asleep & dreaming of a crush. But Hello Kitty lived in heaven, and my mother and I were not in heaven. We were in the San Fernando Valley, the porn capital. And on the way to Mass every Sunday, we would drive by houses with swimming pools where money shots were being made.

BENJAMÍN NAKA-HASEBE KINGSLEY

JESUS IN A JAR OF MAYONNAISE

"Why
they call it *Miracle*   *Whip*"   my daughter
age four   chops her hands
she a real know-it-all
like she's fixing to put   this motherless kitchen
back in order

"Why
don't you watch me
turn this Whip   into wine"   I'll say
anything gets   her smiling

"Like Jesus?" my daughter
inhales   as if she just found sanctification
at the bottom   of this conversation's cereal box

You think Jesus in that jar of mayonnaise?

My mother said God ain't   have no white   man's face
but I still picture him white as mayonnaise   some fool
lifting him up   that sour wine   that vinegary sponge
on a tree branch sayin   "here boy   drink"

So that night I pick up   Nutella for supper
we spread it around real   thick   our ham
cheese sandwiches   proper
dripping No   substitutionary soybean oil   egg   vinegar
water

Nutella is a miracle   says my daughter

"Yea mama" I say back

DUY DOAN

ALLEGORY FOR FAMILY MEMBERS

Bà Ngoại, who will pray for me
when you are gone?

      the master of ceremonies with her microphone

      a young child making hand
      shadows over palm
      leaves during a sermon

      the braids of a toy mare

      the mare

Did my confession make us closer? I killed the pope. Huddled
next to you, burrowed along your side, face down in supplication:
I'm ruined, I've been corrupted forever, Bà Ngoại. When you
told everyone I was your favorite, was this before or after I
confessed? One's the prodigal son, the other is his brother. Either
story works for me. On my birthday, too many lines and the pope
dies.

      guilt, Catholic gifts

      red and gold paper
      packets wasted on games

      the green banana ripening

      red dust lining the lip of the new year's vase

WENDY CHIN-TANNER

ADVENT

ever green
who waits four
Sundays for

the end of
the year clear
brisk air of

night the moon
a small ball
in passing

empurpling
a stripe of
vaulted black

sky a wreath
of the sun's
shadow light

reflection
of a star
you are dust

the dust you
tell yourself
of some dead

star staring
back to see
how far you

have fallen

AMY UYEMATSU

ZAP #30

not one to say prayers
my church with no name
considers all forms
of the sacred

but it takes cancer
to zap my heart
in a way impossible
for me to know before

now blessings arrive
in orchids and cards
the lighting of candles
a home-cooked meal

the generosity of cousins
who ask if they can
include me
at evening grace

the healing secrets
of mystics
a Sikh and his wife
holding each of my hands

and some ancient beliefs
a Mayan frog from Luis
standing guard within
my garden of stones

ADEEBA SHAHID TALUKDER

CLOT

A man pulled his wrist
      to his torso. There, Gabriel learned
         to long.

The air towards God was black.
      Eyelids heavy, a large cloth on His head.
         His wings
      both ends of the sky.

He shook like a leaf.
Squeezed, found
      no drop of blood.

SU HWANG

WHEN STREETS ARE PAVED WITH GOLD

Turn a page from the Dead
        Sea divide to memorize
revised prayers—deliver
        unseen deities. Learn to
say *faith* in sundry
        idioms. Or, lift your head
to map the confederacy
        of lies—weight shifting on
bended knee pressed against
        fallow soil. Removed
from points of origin—gritty
        hands clamor for remedy.
Dirt lodged under nails:
        conspiracy of labor & migrant
colonies; camphor winds &
        lonesome concessions.
Martyrdom hemorrhages
        like a failed birth:
we are made to succumb
        through the centuries.
Same old story, like
        unraveling spools
of roses—a maze. So what
        is the meaning of this,
a proxy to youth? Where
        there can be no mercy, no
grace? Hallelujah.
        Amen, amen.

W. TODD KANEKO

DISBELIEF

If you believe in home, you have to
believe in ghosts in their natural states—

sad-faced and cloaked in magpies because
that's what it means to be residue, shimmer

and fade like fitful sleep. You can forget
how life feels like death only noisier,

how death feels like a whale's song
and skeleton. If you believe in home,

you have to acknowledge that your house
is at least partially fashioned of horse

hide and barbed wire. You can hate
the way the water takes forever

to heat, how there is too much street
light, too little sun in the yard, but notice

your great grandmother at the kitchen table,
her face turned inside out. She can't see

her husband holding up the staircase,
knees buckling, back bent at impossible

angles while outside the crows gather
in the pine trees. They call out to all

of us with frightened voices:
a lullaby, a serenade, a funeral song.

NEIL AITKEN

PRODIGAL

Here is a grief grown white as the moon tonight,
so round with yearning
                    your mother has no more words.

She will not say she has come alone to the shore again
to draw something from the dark echo of waves—

some memory of you as a boy with impossibly small hands.
You with hair that will not part. You curled in the space
between bodies like a small bulb of light.

Not how you left, so awkward and pained,
your want as deep as the fear in your knees,
as the regret in the hollowed bones beneath your skin

or that betraying hand, the one that trembled at your side
by the last needle wound. Your eyes now as still as pebbles
laid in the river bed with no memory of mountains or shores.

She cannot say hell, cannot whisper God,
or even the grave and its diligent worms. What is belief then?
What is faith? If she lets these go, what then?

We want what we cannot see, the other face of the moon,
the one missing. The one turned away at this precise moment.

We want to see, but it is dark in here, in the small narrow world.
It is dark always, then someone opens a door.
Then another. Then another.

There are more rooms than two in the world beyond.
Somewhere her son is sleeping.

BRYNN SAITO

AFTERLIFE

She likes to imagine the afterlife as a coffee shop on 23rd street,
sun streaming through the lettered windows, a loose, midday
wind. She walks in and sees her love sitting in the corner reading
a book about physics. Beside them: a stack of texts—books on
sweetgrass and galaxies, Dickinson's poetry, Davis' letters, books
on teaching and how to be tender inside the machine. They sit
for a while with their coffee and coffee shop music—soft, city-
like, slightly inspirational. Maybe her mother walks in, beaming,
and sits beside them at a table she pulls a few inches closer;
maybe her father joins with his city maps; and her grandmothers
and grandfathers; and her little sister, sober now. Maybe the
coffee shop fills with other people—people she knew briefly who
gave her life meaning: former students, fellow writers, the ones
she met at meditation centers in mountain villages, people she
sat beside on trains barreling through the great and dying cities
of the west. The shop hums with perfect conversation—caffeine-
fueled, laughter-filled, political-spiritual, questioning. She, in the
corner, loves the sound of warm talking and grounded wonder.
The pitch of it brings her a happiness she has always known.

EUGENIA LEIGH

WHAT I MISS MOST ABOUT HELL

is prayer.
I'd pack a plastic bottle

with vodka, drive
to the crag of my life—

the parking lot of a pancake house—
and scream. I prayed

like everyone I loved was on fire.
The bright, violet blob

I called God
would forgive the atrocities

roared in ethanol rage
while I'd shake like a dog

demanding answers
from the maker of figs:

why the sycamore fruit
sweetens only when bruised,

the way a fist will
ripen a child.

KAVEH AKBAR

DESPITE MY EFFORTS EVEN MY PRAYERS HAVE TURNED INTO THREATS

Holy father I can't pretend
I'm not afraid to see you again
but I'll say that when the time
comes I believe my courage
will expand like a sponge
cowboy in water. My earth-
father was far braver than me—
coming to America he knew
no English save Rolling Stones
lyrics and how to say *thanks
God.* Will his goodness roll
over to my tab and if yes, how
soon? I'm sorry for neglecting
your myriad signs, which seem
obvious now as a hawk's head
on an empty plate. I keep waking
up at the bottom of swimming
pools, water reflecting
whatever I miss most: whiskey-
glass, pill bottles, my mother's
oleander, which was sweet
and evergreen but toxic in all
its parts. I know it was silly
to keep what I kept from you;
you've always been so charmed
by my weakness. I just figured
you were becoming fed up with
all your making, like a virtuoso
trying not to smash apart her
flute onstage. Plus, my sins
were practically devotional:
two peaches stolen from
a bodega, so sweet I savored

even the bits I flossed out
my teeth. I know it's no excuse,
but even thinking about them
now I'm drooling. Consider
the night I spent reading
another man's lover the *Dream
Songs* in bed—we made it to
"a green living / drops
limply" before we were
tangled into each other, cat
still sleeping at our feet. Allow
me these treasures, Lord.
Time will break what doesn't
bend—even time. Even you.

I WILL UNLOCK THE LATCH OF THESE LIPS AND PRAISE:
POEMS ABOUT PRAYER AND RITUAL

TINA CHANG

ASCENSION

After checking his pockets
for nickels and dimes, she rubbed
wet cloth upon cloth
until the dirt drifted like a gray spill

of floating cells, faintly alive, bubbling up
for her pruned fingers to touch.
That same year I was baptized.
I drank Holy water from a marble dish,

licked the droplets off my fingers.
Then I took the wafer in my mouth,
letting it shrivel before landing
in my stomach like a divine bullet.

She took his rosary beads from a hook
by the mirror and placed them inside
the dresser among pushpins, unworn
scarves, tubes of chalky lipstick.

She had stopped saying her prayers.
After morning mass, she'd wait for me
across the street. Nights. She locked the door
to the washroom, holding herself steady

over a sink. Her tears dripped into the rust-caked
valves. Mother washed him well when he died.
She cleaned the places that one could easily
forget: the backs of his knees, his chaffed heels,

the soft spaces between his legs. She even scoured
the inside of his mouth with a child's toothbrush.
By then his body had gone completely to bone.
I think of the Christ I saw in watercolors

in Catechism books all the Sundays of my life.
How I studied His body, the way it shined
when He was removed from a tilted cross.
Even as He lay twisted and naked, His spine

spiraling to the mud there was a cluster
of red winged angels reaching toward Him
from the ledge of a cloud and how Mary,
His mother, clung to the mortal shell, her lips

sinking into His collar bone, fingers tightening
around the blue face as His soul stormed
over the ladder of His ribs.

SARAH GAMBITO

OLD DOMINION

When I was born,

the woman ahead of me

had a lovely Om and it was

an Apostle. Children sang around

me and I sang Edelweiss, Nothing but

the Blood and come cookie stick.

In my church, I petted

my spine. I was furry

and luxuriant. Grass growing

nearer. I stood among my conifers

and when no one was

looking I played every character

in the Nativity. I liked it

best when I was Mary

freezing at night.

I kissed the top of

my dollbaby's head while

cars peeled in fleur de lis

around me.

Sarah Gambito

My church

was tall and level-headed.

My church memorized

scripture and made peachy

fingernails and emotional

outbursts in school.

MICHELLE PEÑALOZA

THREAD RITE

I pluck silver and white hairs from Lola's head,
each one for a penny,
as she sits at her Singer.
Bridesmaids' dresses and wedding gowns
drape from the ceiling,
down from hooks meant for hanging plants.

Sundays, beneath Santo Niño and Santa Maria,
beneath the flaming, thorned heart of Christ,
Lola and I and her altars and her trilling Singer.
She pieces together lined panels of gowns
while I pull triplets of silver and white from thick black.

Triplets of silver and white, easy to find in the altar light.
Her hair smells like simmering sinigang.
She and Ma whisper fierce, below Santo Niño's painted eyes,
words I do not know.
I will buy a jawbreaker with the pennies Lola will pay me.

I don't remember their words, only their cross faces.
Their mouths move quick, twisting in ire;
these faces, someday, my mother and I will make.
We will twist our mouths, angry lines stifled—
saying and not saying what we mean.

Lola hums.
White and silver hairs gather upon satin—
ruby, coral, cerulean—
leftover from finished gowns.
My fingertips massage her crown.
Lola hums a song from her throat to her skull to my fingers.

Each errant hair I pluck: a line in a sketch in a dream
where we divine patterns upon red shantung.

The song she will sing. The room where she will die.
Ma will ask everything aloud. Lola will not answer.
We wait for thread and needle, for the Singer, for satin
and sinigang, for shears.

We watch her confusion during dialysis.
Ma and I whisper fierce in the midst of her begging.
Lola asks me to pluck her weak bones, her kidneys.
She will pay me with pennies taken from mason jars.
I sit with her—each time she is sewn, pieced together,
needles going in and out,
as Santo Niño and unfinished wedding dresses watched.

Each hair a line we divined in a sketch in a dream—
a path leading, a cord binding, a rope to pull,
a sheet to cover, a handkerchief to wipe blood and tears.
Ma's triplets of silver and white multiply each time I see her.
I pluck her silver and white hairs, each one for a penny.

OLIVER DE LA PAZ

DEAR EMPIRE,

This is your church. The people bow their heads, almost touching the backs of the people in front of them. They move with the vicar's hands, the way the faces of daisies move towards sun. From up close, the vicar's collar has a stain. His voice box strains against its edge.

The high ceilings arch, making the sound of a slight cough bounce from one end to the other. Sound keeps all in place. There are blue eyes mounted high above in the leaded windows. Light from them is cast down on the heads of those praying. They look like they are swimming, bent the way they are. They look swept.

OLIVER DE LA PAZ

DEAR EMPIRE,

This is your reliquary. In this jar, a knucklebone. And here, a skull with gemstones for teeth. The canines of it shine so that light lashes forth. Its smile bends the beams. From it, emerald light strikes the tabernacle. And lo, it too illuminates.

Blessed be those who are smote by the light of its countenance. Blessed be them. As god speaks, the terrible imposition of his glare shuts the eyes of believers settled in the pews.

And here the silver tourniquets of martyrs. Remnants of their collared bodies dangle from the columns of this holy house. This one lacks a femur. His bones fused by wire. And this one's sternum drips with wax. There are candles lit from inside his ribcage. See its light? See how all their bodies glow?

MARCI CALABRETTA CANCIO-BELLO

INVOCATION

Lord, I have pulled myself up this mountainside to burn
a thousand days of incense, laden with ginseng wine to pour
on the pitted feet of this stone servant of yours.
My prayer is stitched in the skin on my side,
over the rib that binds me to men—to husband, to son.
Here will I sit and kneel and beg to know what you can spare

and who you will not. My mother, who left the sea unspared,
who culled creature from wave, who burns
coal for the shrimp and the clams and the pigs, who seasons
nothing but wine, whole roots of ginseng blocking my pores—
spare her. Spare my husband, who razes tiny forests inside
his bonsai room, reshaping the branches, believing you

reshape us after death to return as stags or sunflowers. Do you?
Do you know how my daughter spreads her scrolls, dabs sparingly—
too sparingly—at the ink, how she renders and flings aside
these tangerines, these sows, how she hungers and burns
for a different shore. For her I curve my spine daily, poring
over ropes of pearls hung loose and swaying in unison

on my wall, iridescent stitchery like whitecaps catching the sun.
This sandalwood burns for her. Only the wine is yours.
Remember how, the second night I gave birth, you poured
out a blessed rain so that the water deer stirred in the sparse
trees outside our window? This turmeric and pine burns
for my son. Remember me, on this same mountainside

many years ago, how I begged and would not subside,
how I offered an oath in exchange for a son,
how the fog curled like a young vine, how it burned
back into the sky like a prayer, how I asked you
what I must give to receive. My own body was not spared
from this oath. What else could I offer, being poor?

Remember me, Lord who was also a son. I have poured
out the last of the wine. Do not take back the rib from my side.
Do not ask in return what was given. Who will you spare,
who not? My mother, my husband, my daughter, my son.
I am here for the reaping. Only this wine is yours.
All of the forest now lifts a prayer with its burning.

Spare my son
or let burn the mountainside.
I have already poured into the dirt what is yours.

RACHELLE CRUZ

HOW TO PRAY

Hayward, California

God loves you on your knees.
Prayers smudged onto the windshield aren't enough.
Tulip bulbs break from soil despite your waiting.
Your mother's mouth as sweet and bitter as a plum.

Prayers smudged onto the windshield aren't enough.
Her knees frozen on a bed of uncooked rice.
Your mother's mouth as sweet and bitter as a plum.
Your broken teeth fail you, now strung into a rosary.

Her knees frozen on a bed of uncooked rice.
Where you won't go: children inspecting stigmata on both feet.
Your broken teeth fail you, now strung into a rosary.
A thief leaves you stinging and penniless.

Where you won't go: children inspecting stigmata on both feet.
What is God's will for monsters anyway?
A thief leaves you stinging and penniless.
Every mother knows that.

What is God's will for monsters anyway?
Look: a heart drawn in Sharpie because here.
Every mother knows that.
You first saw glare but God in every window.

Look: a heart drawn in Sharpie because here.
Mystery is the pilot-light behind your navel.
You first saw glare but God in every window.
Humming theme songs and jingles, prayer.

Mystery is the pilot-light behind your navel.
Your mother's silence is good with your names.

Humming theme songs and jingles, prayer.
Beloved monster, nose pressed to the porch screen.

Your mother's silence is good with your names.
Tulip bulbs break from soil despite your waiting.
Beloved monster, nose pressed to the porch screen.
God loves you on your knees.

EILEEN R. TABIOS

THE SECRET LIFE OF AN ANGEL

after José Garcia Villa's "Girl Singing"

Girl singing. Day. The old man

of winter reaches for immortality
with a lengthening shadow
despite my skipping away.

Girl singing! I insist. Day!
I chant like the Babaylan I will
become to keep the clouds

from dimming the sun, from
milking the sky of its cobalt
gaze. He has worn many

disguises, and I have let him:
the original angel who fell
and fell. "It's a glorious ride,"

he has whispered as part of his
spell. "This is a game of poker
I have lost, but no longer wish

to play," I reply. Girl singing.
Day. I insist and proclaim:
"You cannot scoff, my secret

demon. For I played with high
stakes while you only watched."
Girl singing. Day. I risked

everything while you hedged
so I could sing notes

only virgin boys can muster,
only fearful dogs can hear.
I lost myself in the 'valley
of evil' but my wings unfurled

to make me rise. Unlike your
wings, mine did not betray—
unfurling as I changed my mind

for Heaven nearer than a breath away.

BARBARA JANE REYES

PSALM FOR MARY JANE VELOSO

Praise the monstrous body, too enormous to describe. When the tongue is taken, how may the mouth even try.

Praise the bitch slapped face, the hemorrhaged eyes. The cluster. The clot. We thin our blood, we run. We run, and we always look back.

Praise the trafficked body, the one that is excised. On smartphones, with hashtags, we lament the phantom part.

Praise the foreign object rushing to the heart. That is you, the help, the heroine. We pump our fists for you, *isang bagsak*!

Praise the ever-present lens, the firing squad shoots every curse and plea. Your breath is a miracle, a lifeline, a headline.

The old you is dead. Praise for her soul. We offer to her our last *Lacrimosa*. Praise the new you, the chrysalis, the secluded saint.

Praise you. May you emerge, graced and gospeled. Unjudged, unfallen, and the color of sky.

EUGENIA LEIGH

PSALM 107

Praise you for that blanket.

Praise you for the stranger
who draped it over my mother,

her naked body perched, pregnant,
in the snow. Praise you
for my father

who said he'd kill her
if she ran. And for my mother,
who didn't run. Like a mannequin
or a stupid dog.

Praise you for her skin
the color of cold
jellyfish, her psalms
careening from her throat
to her belly, where your fingers—

praise your fingers—forged
my unformed body. Praise you
for my bloodline. For the savages
and the idiots, whom you love
the same. Thank you
for the bones you stacked in me

to brave this unsettling.

SHANKAR NARAYAN

PSALM FROM THE OLD WORLD

Praise the dragonfly
that levitates like a drone
above your Red Sea.

Praise the drone
that machinates my manna
through layers of unbreathed air
to drop dead at my feet.

Praise the mother-
board implementing for me
emotions I never grasped
I needed so precisely.

Praise the father-
land who makes void
for me and for dragonflies
and inserts us both into the annals
of the server farm.

But most of all, praise you, intelligence
without name, praise you for filling
the form that does not exist
before I ever see it, and for knowing
what I want before I know
I want it, and for delivering to me

dragonflies, houseflies, box flies,
tarantulae, various arthropods and mollusks,
including octopuses with flagellating tentacles
and infinite suckers, and the knowledge
that there truly are no octopi,

and sperm whales and spider goats and aggregates

of white cats engaged in binary pursuits such as vole
hunting, dog torture, and accurately random
somersaults, and the Burj Dubai, and DNA
scissors, not to mention microcosms of myriad
individual deaths by drowning, boiling, bombing,
pollution, artifice, ennui, or benign neglect—

praise you without artifice
who are unseen but sees me
eyeless, you see all of me in time
transcend my own flesh, risen in silicon
from the waters' unsteady meniscus,
and out into a perfected world

without flesh

and without
water.

VIKAS MENON

PRAYER FOR THE RENDING

> "Protect us with your spear, O Devi, protect us
> with your sword O Ambika".
> **—Devi Mahatmya**

You who severed the stem of the apple

that startled Newton's skull,
met Eve's half-open, expectant lips—

You who seared words
into Oppenheimer's brain—

O Breath of Breaths,
my ever silent kin—

what more penance do You
need than this:

tonight, a mother boils stones
in water as her children

await their rice, biding her time
and all the while praying to you

O Beloved Scythe,
Sweet Thief—

let them fall asleep
let them fall asleep

SUN YUNG SHIN

NAMES BETWEEN THE HOLES | LACING THE DEAD FATHER

Father,

Now I have to rename you.

Let us walk through the breaking snow together.

Our inheritance is the air resting on my palm.

The period is my fingerprint.

I found your names on the ground:

.Talc.
.Undressed.
.Ink.
.Divided.
.Mineral.
.Morphine.
.United.
.Dressed.
.Black rosary.
.Wreath.
.Sisters.
.Ribbon.
.Temple.
.Gods.
.Hours.
.Coal.
.Cave.
.Fire.
.Smoke.
.Skull.
.Diamond.

.Porcelain.

.Afterbirth.

.Corridor.

.Spear.

.Ship.

.Wake.

.Agate.

.Moonlight.

.Milky quartz.

.Eye.

.Island.

.Undertow.

VANDANA KHANNA

PRAYER TO RECOGNIZE THE BODY

There must be a word for this
heart-growing, to explain

these teeth, stinging like a gift—
tremble of sweat coaxed from scalp

and flesh. The next thing I covet:
the third eye's velvet blink, the green

pulse in my veins of a forest
I can't make myself step

out of. And what of all the things
remade, swabbed free of salt?

Because who can tell the difference
in the dark between antlers and branches

and bone, between the thick-haired
chest of an animal and you?

MIA AYUMI MALHOTRA

PSALM

I will unlatch the lock
of these lips and praise,

press them to the crack
of light as it widens

in the jamb, a hand
filled, now flowing.

How I long for bread.
This body, its greed,

the ache I carry under
hasp and key, trapdoor

sealed, now sprung.
Called to stand on

ragged knees, pebbles
cast into a still face.

Take it. Take it all—
wet, waiting mouth.

KATHLEEN HELLEN

THE WAY OF TEA

Coarse or finer substance matters.

Attend to how the thistle and camellia
picked that morning stand arranged,
how early evening wind ruffles the scroll,
how light infuses sorrow.

Put the kettle on to sigh.
Sprinkle water at the gate to let him know you are ready.
Let him leave his sandals at the door.

Bow, and when the door is softly closed
level powder, scoop the water to the bowl
with your finger at the joint.

Name the ladle cup of moon.
Name the mouth the taking.

Distinguish every sweetness.
Say, this is the only sweetness.

PURVI SHAH

AT THE EDGE OF HER BANGLE, SARASWATI RECKONS WITH THE ONE FLAME

"The very mentioning of Hindu sacred thread ceremony (Upanayan), a Vedic practice, for a girl or woman will cause a flutter among orthodox Hindus and traditionalists. For the conservatives, sacred thread ceremony is only for boys and men. But Sejal Amod Ketkar, eight-year-old girl from Thane, went through the sacred initiation rite and the ceremony was performed by a female priest as male priests were not ready to perform the ritual on a girl."

–Abhilash Rajendran, "Hindu Sacred Thread Ceremony (Upanayan) for Girl Child – Breaking Traditions for Good," Hindu Blog, May 29, 2009

Is fire not pure?

First, anoint me black

bangle shimmering

Third: do not attest

flame. Darken infinity —

us of a match

in the glint of a girl's

wit & raised head. Second:

adorn

your shoulder as though you never burnished thread.

just the to-be-men had claim to

our wrist horizon — let sunrise remind

at the household altar — how these marble

gods tender at our everyday's grace. With

Purvi Shah

a fistful

of grains,

crocus, neem

leaves & a blanket

of marigold slivers,

blaze

our dreams upright, perfect that circle

of sacred

flesh, seek

succor

in round sound

of metal to metal,

two hands clinking wrists, two hands

marking story & history, two hands

dancing creation & its return. After

such reckoning, blossom

Purvi Shah

then child, string resonance,

unbend circle, spark alphabets

in the air; filigree syllables as fierce

mettle — sound your fiery god

-praise.

KAZIM ALI

DIVINATION

Square and circle my neat birth chart impresses

Drawn to separate a single clear note emerging

From a wash of ambient sound of stars and planets

Individual notes discrete revolve around the sun

Here I am a threaded bead impaled by decades

By prayers I can't see or hear but slide along the thread

Neither the one praying nor the prayer itself

Just a clot of muscle and bone counting

I spin how clouds condense amber from the tree

Driftwood on the Baltic smooth under the palm

All roughness eroded on a map of the mountain's ridges

In color liken themselves to some other place

Algeria rhymes with Paraguay or Taiwan and Morocco with
    Chile or Bhutan

Confusion and utterance

South wind southern

Shuttered shut torn as per usual

Devil and his split tongue gives a word as another word

In the generalife of the Alhambra we saw an Arab couple with
  their lonely planet guide

And the cypress tree leaning over

It may have witnessed the assignation but it looks dead to me

How much we want to hold on to history

I want to hold in my arms

My many lives

The one when I flew with blue wings

Or when I was on my back covered in sculptor's dust

Or when I spied the Arab couple with a guide book in Hebrew

Or the time in the grey city I wanted to strangle myself

With flowers and mist stoking infernos in my rib cage

Reading the *Master Letters* in the coffee shop of the bus station

Solid cold sky wet on my skin

My chest a prisoned cathedral

Never told in the park the winter brought

I am forgotten how to draw myself

In ice on the glass that no one told shattered

Chapters of tinsel dark lust and angry loneliness

I disappeared then amidst thrum and hunger

If you want to know the edge of ocean or sky

Water and air unloosens itself

Pitched into the season of orange

No weapon but green

I lost myself in the sedimented time of petrified woods

You are a door leading nowhere in the slopes of ardor and crime

Heretics used to burn

Your heresy is you believe the body has a mind and a spirit too

That it is a ladder to god

That bones and muscle are

Bricks of Babel

Of course you could try to actually look at yourself

Lie and say so casually oh it just came to me in the rain

I put a jacket of mist and flowers in my suitcase

All the contracts of lethargy and forgetfulness

I've refused to sign and on the other side of the glass

A friend I don't recognize, the brave one

Who unpacked all my shirts of silence

And now who am I without them

Kazim Ali

When I open my mouth

There's nothing left inside

I am only myself to throw now, grown into bell and ghost garden
    bird

Third every night to soar

Petals in my mouth

I want a big pocketful of coins now

Cents crazy you will be and festooned

Yes I is you

The papers are all writing stories about you

It's the now that will be your lover

Stripped in summer suck

Stringed to the sky wingless

You will be a knot of cleverness

This crime is my second offense

Accordion to conventional wisdom

The wind that carries the siren-song landwards

A land word land bridge my second or third try

Ken you quickly tell me

Ken you quickly kell me

When I thought up logos I foundered

Old ghost caused almost

There built I in the roots of the earth

A stone laboratory my labor labial

Pronounce a nonce announce

I can't spell your sin

Spill to the rest

To the west the third most important shrine

To color always counting god by shade

This flower book dehisces not close to you

Feeling in wonder through

The powder of gold air flouring

Fleet that sluices through

You sailed yourself to the end of vision

You spent are spent passed hand in hand

Lust spawn sent in throes of flower

Now petal yourself astronomical

Sky flower throw your voice of light

Petal yourself labialalluvial

Kazim Ali

Soaked clear through luminous spent

Kneeling before intensity why should the vessel be always unscathed

Why should the I always be spared

Don't you want to know you have been passed through

HYEJUNG KOOK

A CONSOLATION: PERMITTING MOURNING

"…it is an impious thing to lament for those whose
souls pass immediately into a better and more divine
state."
                    –Plutarch, "Consolatio ad Uxorem"

Bewildered, be wilder, freely
weep, weep, weep, weep,
            weep since we cannot burn
the pyre for one who never
        was born, only quickened
                then left us without a body.
Wearing white hemp or black,
        refuse to look skyward for weeks.
Give grief its honors, risk
        its rooting into the threshold,
the necessity of tearing down
    lintels, walls askew ever after.
            I'll mend the breaks with lacquer
and gold, never mind my lack
        of skill, clay, rat-hair brush.
Wind wailing, the work will hold.
    In daylight, my rough joins
                will glimmer and flash.

MIA AYUMI MALHOTRA

ONE DAY YOU'LL LOOK IN THE MIRROR AND SEE LIONS

May you not fear what lies ahead.
    May the moon's full face
        light your own, milky
with tears. May it ferry you into mystery.
    May your body, luminous
        in its skin, so thin the bones
           glow through, brim
        with whispered prayers,
lacrimal and lesser wings.

May the lion's mouth be shut.
    May its head sink to the ground
        at your approach, splendid
    in your cotton nightie, an apparition
of joint and socket plainly revealed.
    May you stand and be spared.
        Please, all I ask.

Cast in greenish light, your hands rise,
    tendril-like, to receive
        a fullness your daughter,
    drawing near, feels spilling
onto her fingers. Poor soul, you can see
        the fear lifting like smoke
off her skin. *Don't fight,* you want to say.
Come, stroke the beast's shaggy head.
    Pull open its terrible maw, see
        for yourself, not the teeth
    you expect, but the gentle rumination
of bovid incisors, muted tongue.
    Come, child. Lie with the lion.
        The ox, the lamb.

NOTES

"Prayer in Writing" and "Allegory for Family Members": "Bà Ngoại"—maternal grandmother

"Mankind is so Fallible" draws from the Charleston church shooting. On June 17, 2015, Dylann Roof, a 21-year-old white supremacist walked into the African Methodist Episcopal Church in South Carolina during prayer service, shot and killed nine people including the church's senior pastor. The church was 201 years old at the time and played a significant role in black history from support during the slavery era, to the Civil Rights Movement, to Black Lives Matter.

"The Secret Life of an Angel": "Babaylan" is an indigenous Filipino religious leader who functions as a healer, a shaman, a seer and a community leader (or any combination of these roles).

"From Dear Blank Space" Excerpted sections are from a longer lyrical piece appearing in *Entropy*, 2015.

- *Dear Wilderness*: Essay referenced is "Bewilderment" by Fanny Howe.

- *Dear Decreation*: Quotation from Tanizaki is from his essay "In Praise of Shadows" (1933). Other quotations are from a video "The Shadow Universe Revealed" by Dennis Overbye, Jonathan Corum and Jason Drakefordin in *The New York Times* (July 15, 2014).

- *Dear Longing*: "The visible world…" is from "Immanence" by Fanny Howe.

"In Defense of Monsters": During the coverage of the March 22, 2017, terrorist attack on Westminster Bridge in London, England, where a man, a self-identified Muslim Briton, killed four people and injured more than fifty by crashing into them with his car, a photograph of an unidentified hijab-wearing Muslim woman walking past a victim while on her cell phone went viral. Many people on social media referred to the woman as a "monster," interpreting her attention to her phone as 124 further evidence that Muslims support terrorism, practice a heartless religion, and feel, at best, indifferent to the carnage perpetrated in "the name of" their/our religion. The epigraph is excerpted from the woman's response to this inflammatory coverage.

CONTRIBUTOR BIOGRAPHIES

Neil Aitken is the author of *Babbage's Dream* (Sundress Publications, 2017) and *The Lost Country of Sight* (Anhinga Press, 2008), winner of the Philip Levine Prize. A past Kundiman poetry fellow, he is the founding editor of *Boxcar Poetry Review*, curator of *Have Book Will Travel*, and host of *The Lit Fantastic* podcast. His own poetry has appeared in *The Adroit Journal, American Literary Review, Crab Orchard Review,* and elsewhere. He presently works as a creative writing coach and serves as co-director of *De-Canon: A Visibility Project*, a library and event space that showcases the work of writers of color.

Kaveh Akbar's poems appear in *The New Yorker, Poetry, Paris Review, Best American Poetry, The New York Times,* and elsewhere. He is the author of two full-length collections: *Pilgrim Bell* (Graywolf, 2021) and *Calling a Wolf a Wolf* (Alice James, 2017). The recipient of a Levis Reading Prize, Pushcart Prizes, and a Ruth Lilly and Dorothy Sargent Rosenberg Poetry Fellowship, Kaveh is the founding editor of *Divedapper*, a home for interviews with major voices in contemporary poetry. Born in Tehran, Iran, he teaches at Purdue University and in the low-residency MFA programs at Randolph College and Warren Wilson.

Kazim Ali was born in the United Kingdom to Muslim parents of Indian, Iranian, and Egyptian descent. He received a B.A. and M.A. from the University of Albany-SUNY, and an M.F.A. from New York University. His books encompass several volumes of poetry, including *Inquisition, Sky Ward*, winner of the Ohioana Book Award in Poetry; *The Far Mosque*, winner of Alice James Books' New England/New York Award; *The Fortieth Day*; *All One's Blue*; and the cross-genre text *Bright Felon*. His novels include the recently published *The Secret Room: A String Quartet* and among his books of essays are the hybrid memoir *Silver Road: Essays, Maps & Calligraphies* and *Fasting for Ramadan: Notes from a Spiritual Practice*. Ali has taught at various colleges and universities, including Oberlin College, Davidson College, St. Mary's College of California, and Naropa University. He is currently a professor of Literature and

Writing at the University of California, San Diego.

Marci Calabretta Cancio-Bello is the author of the poetry collection *Hour of the Ox* (University of Pittsburgh, 2016), which won the 2015 AWP Donald Hall Prize and a 2016 Florida Book Award, and was a finalist for the 2017 Milt Kessler Award. She has received poetry fellowships from Kundiman, the Knight Foundation, and the American Literary Translators Association, among others. Her work has appeared in *Best New Poets*, *Best Small Fictions*, *The New York Times*, and more. She serves as a program coordinator for Miami Book Fair. www.marcicalabretta.com.

Marianne Chan grew up in Stuttgart, Germany, and Lansing, Michigan. She is the author of *All Heathens*, forthcoming from Sarabande Books in 2020. Her poems have appeared or are forthcoming in *Cincinnati Review*, *Indiana Review*, *West Branch*, *The Journal*, *The Rumpus*, and elsewhere. She holds an MFA from the University of Nevada, Las Vegas, and is currently pursuing a PhD in Creative Writing at the University of Cincinnati.

K-Ming Chang is a Lambda Literary Award finalist. Her debut novel is forthcoming from One World / Random House. Her poems can be found in *Poetry*, *The Margins*, and *Poem-A-Day*. She is located at www.kmingchang.com and on Twitter @k_mingchang.

Tina Chang is an American poet, teacher, and editor. In 2010, she was the first woman to be named Poet Laureate of Brooklyn. She is the author of three poetry collections: *Hybrida* (W. W. Norton, May 2019), *Of Gods & Strangers* (Four Way Books, 2011), and *Half-Lit Houses* (Four Way Books, 2004). She is also the co-editor of the seminal anthology *Language for a New Century: Contemporary Poetry from the Middle East, Asia, and Beyond* (W.W. Norton, 2008).

Jennifer S. Cheng is the author of *MOON: Letters, Maps, Poems*, selected by Bhanu Kapil for the Tarpaulin Sky Book Award and named a *Publishers Weekly* "Best Book of 2018"; *House A*, selected by Claudia Rankine for the Omnidawn Poetry Book Prize; and *Invocation: An Essay*, an image-text chapbook. She is a 2019 National

Endowment for the Arts Fellow and received support and awards from Brown University, the University of Iowa, the U.S. Fulbright program, Kundiman, Bread Loaf, and the Academy of American Poets. Having grown up in Texas and Hong Kong, she lives in San Francisco. www.jenniferscheng.com.

Wendy Chin-Tanner is the author of the poetry collections *Turn* (SRP, 2014), which was a finalist for the Oregon Book Award, and *Anyone Will Tell You*, (SRP, 2019). She is a poetry editor at *The Nervous Breakdown* and co-publisher at *A Wave Blue World*, an independent publishing company for graphic novels. Some of her poems can be found at *RHINO, Denver Quarterly, The Rumpus, Vinyl, The Collagist, North Dakota Quarterly*, and *The Mays Anthology of Oxford and Cambridge*. A trained sociologist specializing in cultural studies, Wendy was born and raised in NYC and educated at Cambridge University, UK.

Rachelle Cruz is from Hayward, California. She is the author of *God's Will for Monsters* (Inlandia, 2017), which won an American Book Award in 2018 and the 2016 Hillary Gravendyk Regional Poetry Prize. She co-edited *Kuwento: Lost Things*, an anthology of Philippine Myths (Carayan Press, 2015) with Melissa Sipin. She hosts *The Blood-Jet Writing Hour* with Muriel Leung. An Emerging Voices Fellow, a Kundiman Fellow and a VONA writer, she lives and writes in Southern California.

Oliver de la Paz is the author of several collections of poetry. His most recent book is *The Boy in the Labyrinth* (University of Akron Press, 2019). He co-edited *A Face to Meet the Faces: An Anthology of Contemporary Persona Poetry*, and serves as the co-chair of the Kundiman advisory board. His work has been published or is forthcoming in journals such as the *New England Review, Tin House*, and *Poetry*. He teaches at the College of the Holy Cross and in the Low Res MFA Program at PLU.

Christian Detisch's poetry and prose has appeared in *Image, Blackbird, Unsplendid, Hyphen* magazine, and elsewhere. He is an MDiv candidate at Yale's Institute of Sacred Music.

Duy Doan is a Vietnamese American poet and the author of *We Play a Game*, selected by Carl Phillips for the Yale Series of Younger Poets Prize. His work has appeared in the Academy of American Poets *Poem-a-Day*, *Poetry*, *Slate*, and *TriQuarterly*. He has been featured in *Poetry* magazine's Editors' Blog and PBS's *Poetry in America*. A Kundiman fellow, he received an MFA in poetry from Boston University. He lives in Austin, Texas.

Christy NaMee Eriksen is an artist, teaching artist, and organizer whose work is grounded in social justice and community engagement. Described as a "tender powerhouse," NaMee blends personal narrative, poetry, and the politics of identity. Her/her work has appeared in such places as Equilibrium at The Loft Literary Center, *The Roundhouse*, and the anthology *Revolutionary Mothering: Love on the Front Lines*. She has received awards for both art and activism, including two Rasmuson Foundation awards, the Equilibrium Spoken Word Immersion Fellowship, Mayor's Award for Artist of the Year and the Carla Tipone Award for Activism.

Tarfia Faizullah is the author of two poetry collections, *Registers of Illuminated Villages* (Graywolf, 2018) and *Seam* (SIU, 2014). Tarfia's writing appears widely in the U.S. and abroad in the *Daily Star*, *Hindu Business Line*, *BuzzFeed*, *PBS News Hour*, *Huffington Post*, *Poetry Magazine*, *Ms. Magazine*, the *Academy of American Poets*, *Oxford American*, the *New Republic*, the *Nation*, *Halal If You Hear Me* (Haymarket, 2019), and has been displayed at the Smithsonian, the Rubin Museum of Art, and elsewhere.

Sarah Gambito is the author of the poetry collections *Loves You*, *Delivered* and *Matadora*. Her honors include the Barnes & Noble Writers for Writers Award from *Poets and Writers*, The Wai Look Award for Outstanding Service to the Arts from the Asian American Arts Alliance and grants and fellowships from The National Endowment for the Arts, The New York Foundation for the Arts and The MacDowell Colony. She is Associate Professor of English / Director of Creative Writing at Fordham University and co-founder of Kundiman, a non-profit organization serving writers and readers of Asian American literature.

Born in Tokyo, half Japanese, **Kathleen Hellen** is the author of *The Only Country was the Color of My Skin* (2018), the award-winning collection *Umberto's Night*, and two chapbooks, *The Girl Who Loved Mothra* and *Pentimento*. Nominated for the Pushcart and *Best of the Net*, and featured on *Poetry Daily*, her poems are widely published and have won the Washington Writers' Publishing House prize, the Thomas Merton poetry prize and prizes from the *H.O.W. Journal* and *Washington Square Review*. For more on Kathleen visit www.kathleenhellen.com.

Leslieann Hobayan is a poet-writer, Jersey girl, and VONA alum. Her work has appeared in *The Rumpus, Aster(ix) Journal, The Lantern Review*, and *The Grief Diaries*, among others, and has been nominated for a Pushcart Prize and 2018 Best of the Net. She has been awarded the James Merrill Fellowship for Poetry at the Vermont Studio Center, a Mid-Atlantic Arts Foundation writing fellowship for a residency at Millay Colony for the Arts, and an artist grant for the Bread Loaf Orion Environmental Writers Conference. She is also a certified yoga instructor who teaches vinyasa, meditation, and Kundalini yoga.

Su Hwang is a poet, activist, and the author of *Bodega* (Milkweed Editions, 2019). Born in Seoul, Korea, she was raised in New York then called the Bay Area home before transplanting to the Midwest. A recipient of the inaugural Jerome Hill Fellowship in Literature, she teaches creative writing with the Minnesota Prison Writing Workshop and is the cofounder, with poet-educator-healer Sun Yung Shin, of Poetry Asylum. Su currently lives in Minneapolis.

W. Todd Kaneko is the author of *The Dead Wrestler Elegies* (Curbside Splendor 2014) and *This Is How the Bone Sings* (Black Lawrence Press 2020), and co-author with Amorak Huey of *Poetry: A Writer's Guide and Anthology* (Bloomsbury Academic 2018). His poetry and prose can be seen in *Alaska Quarterly Review, Massachusetts Review, The Normal School, Barrelhouse, The Rumpus, Best Small Fictions 2017* and *2018*, and many other journals and anthologies. A Kundiman fellow, he is co-editor of *Waxwing* magazine and lives in

Grand Rapids, Michigan where he teaches at Grand Valley State University.

Totem: America (Tiger Bark, 2018) is **Debra Kang Dean's** third and most recent full-length collection of poetry. Her poems have been featured on *Poetry Daily*, *Verse Daily*, and on the Academy of America Poets' Poem-a-Day website. Her essays are included in the expanded edition of *The Colors of Nature: Culture, Identity, and the Natural World* (Milkweed, 2011) and in *Until Everything Is Continuous Again: American Poets on the Work of W. S. Merwin* (WordFarm, 2014). She was born and raised in Hawai'i and is on the faculty of Spalding University's School of Creative and Professional Writing.

Born in New Delhi, India, **Vandana Khanna** is a writer, educator, and editor. She is the author of two collections of poetry: *Train to Agra* and *Afternoon Masala*, as well as the chapbook, *The Goddess Monologues*. Her poems have won the Crab Orchard Review First Book Prize, The Miller Williams Poetry Prize, and the Diode Editions Chapbook Competition. Her work has been published widely in journals and anthologies such as the Academy of American Poets' *Poem-a-Day*, *New England Review*, *The Missouri Review*, *Raising Lilly Ledbetter: Women Poets Occupy the Workspace*, and *Indivisible: An Anthology of Contemporary South Asian American Poetry*.

Hei Kyong Kim (aka Beth Kyong Lo) was adopted from Seoul, South Korea in 1975. By day she works as a clinical psychologist and by night she writes creatively. Her first collection of poetry and prose, *The Translation of Han*, was released in June 2014 by CQT Publishing and Media. Her additional work can be found in numerous journals and anthologies, including *Parenting as Adoptees*, *Outsiders Within*, *Seeds from a Silent Tree*, *Paj Ntaub Voice*, *Journal of Asian American Renaissance*, *New Truths: Writing in the 21st Century by Korean Adoptees*, *MoonRoot*, and *How Dare We! Write*.

E. J. Koh is a poet and translator in Seattle, WA. She earned her MFA from Columbia University and is completing her PhD at the University of Washington in English Language and Literature. Her first book of poetry *A Lesser Love* was the winner of the Pleiades

Editors Prize and published in 2017. Her memoir *The Magical Language of Others* is forthcoming from Tin House Books. Her poems, translations, and stories have appeared in *Boston Review, Los Angeles Review of Books, Prairie Schooner, World Literature Today,* and others. She is the recipient of The MacDowell Colony fellowship and the 2017 ALTA Emerging Translator Mentorship.

Hyejung Kook's poetry has appeared in *The Massachusetts Review, Glass: A Journal of Poetry, Hyphen* magazine, *Pleiades, Verse Daily, Beloit Poetry Journal,* the *Denver Quarterly,* and elsewhere. Other works include an essay in *The Critical Flame* and a chamber opera libretto. Hyejung was born in Seoul, Korea, grew up in Pennsylvania, and now lives in Kansas with her husband and their two children. She is a Fulbright grantee and a Kundiman fellow.

Jennifer Kwon Dobbs is the author of the poetry collections *Paper Pavilion* (White Pine Press Poetry Prize 2007), *Interrogation Room* (White Pine Press 2018), and the chapbooks *Notes from a Missing Person* (Essay Press 2013) and *Necro Citizens* (hochroth Verlag, German and English 2019). Currently co-editing *Radical Kinships: An Anthology of Autocritical Writing* and working on a third poetry collection on settler colonial kitsch, she is associate professor of creative writing and program director of Race and Ethnic Studies at St. Olaf College.

Ed Bok Lee is the author of three books of poetry, most recently *Mitochondrial Night* (Coffee House Press, 2019). The son of North and South Korean emigrants—his mother originally a refugee from what is now North Korea; his father was raised during the Japanese colonial period and Korean War in what is now South Korea—Lee grew up in South Korea, North Dakota, and Minnesota, and was educated there and later on both U.S. coasts, Russia, South Korea, and Kazakhstan. He teaches at Metropolitan State University in Saint Paul, and also works as an artist, translator, and for two decades has taught in programs for youth and the incarcerated. Honors include an American Book Award, Minnesota Book Award, Asian American Literary Award (Members' Choice), and a PEN/Open Book Award.

Contributor Biographies

Li-Young Lee is the author of five books of poetry, including his newest collection, *The Undressing*. His earlier collections are *Behind My Eyes*; *Book of My Nights*; *Rose*, winner of the Delmore Schwartz Memorial Award; *The City in Which I Love You*, the 1990 Lamont Poetry Selection; and a memoir entitled *The Winged Seed: A Remembrance*, which received an American Book Award from the Before Columbus Foundation and reissued by BOA Editions in 2012. Lee's honors include fellowships from the National Endowment for the Arts, The Lannan Foundation, and the John Simon Guggenheim Memorial Foundation, as well as grants from the Illinois Arts Council, the Commonwealth of Pennsylvania, and the Pennsylvania Council on the Arts.

Joseph O. Legaspi is the author of the poetry collections *Threshold* and *Imago*, both from CavanKerry Press; and three chapbooks: *Postcards* (Ghost Bird Press), *Aviary, Bestiary* (Organic Weapon Arts), and *Subways* (Thrush Press). Recent works have appeared in *POETRY*, *New England Review*, *World Literature Today*, *Best of the Net* and the anthology *Reel Verse* (Everyman's Library). He cofounded Kundiman (www.kundiman.org), a national nonprofit organization dedicated to nurturing generations of writers and readers of Asian American literature. He lives with his husband in Queens, New York.

Eugenia Leigh is a Korean American poet and the author of *Blood, Sparrows and Sparrows* (Four Way Books), the winner of the 2015 Debut-litzer Prize in Poetry and a finalist for both the National Poetry Series and the Yale Series of Younger Poets. Her poems and essays have appeared in numerous publications including *The Rumpus*, *North American Review*, and the *Best New Poets 2010* anthology. The recipient of fellowships and awards from *Poets & Writers Magazine*, Kundiman, The Frost Place, *Rattle*, and the *Asian American Literary Review*, Eugenia received her MFA from Sarah Lawrence College.

Kenji C. Liu is the author of *Monsters I Have Been* (Alice James Books 2019), and *Map of an Onion*, national winner of the 2015 Hillary Gravendyk Poetry Prize. His poetry can be found, among other places, in *American Poetry Review*, *Anomaly*, *The Feminist Wire*, *Gulf Coast*, Split This Rock's poem of the week series, several anthologies, and two chapbooks, *Craters: A Field Guide* (2017) and *You Left Without Your Shoes* (2009). A Kundiman fellow and an alumnus of VONA/Voices, the Djerassi Resident Artist Program, and the Community of Writers, he lives in Los Angeles and is a member of the Miresa Collective.

Timothy Liu is the author of ten books of poems, including the forthcoming *Luminous Debris: New and Selected Legerdemain, 1992-2017*. He lives in Manhattan and Woodstock, NY. www.timothyliu. net.

Shireen Madon's poetry has appeared in or is forthcoming from *Indiana Review*, *Prairie Schooner*, *Poetry Northwest*, *Hayden's Ferry Review*, *The Greensboro Review*, and *The Margins*, among others. A Kundiman fellow, she has been the recipient of an Amy Award from Poets & Writers and a Bennet Poetry Prize from the Academy of American Poets.

Mia Ayumi Malhotra is the author of *Isako Isako* (Alice James Books, 2018), winner of the Alice James Award, the Nautilus Gold Award for Poetry, a National Indie Excellence Award, and a Maine Literary Award. She holds a BA from Stanford University and an MFA from the University of Washington, and her poetry has appeared in numerous literary journals and anthologies, including *The Yale Review*, *CALYX*, *Indiana Review*, and *Ink Knows No Borders: Poems of the Immigrant and Refugee Experience*. A Pushcart Prize nominee and a founding editor of Lantern Review, Mia has received fellowships from the VONA/Voices Writing Workshop and Kundiman, an organization dedicated to the cultivation of Asian American writing. She currently lives in the San Francisco Bay Area.

Vikas K. Menon is a poet, playwright and songwriter. He was a 2015 Emerging Poets Fellow at Poets House and his poems have been featured in numerous publications, including *The HarperCollins Book of English Poetry*. He co-wrote *Priya's Shakti* (www.

priyashakti.com), the first of a series of ongoing augmented reality comic books that address gender-based violence. He was one of the co-writers of the shadowplay *Feathers of Fire: A Persian Epic* which has had 112 performances worldwide. He is currently an Advisory Board Member of Kundiman, dedicated to nurturing generations of writers and readers of Asian American literature.

Rajiv Mohabir is the author of *The Cowherd's Son* (Tupelo Press, 2017, winner of the 2015 Kundiman Prize) and *The Taxidermist's Cut* (Four Way Books, 2016, winner of the Four Way Books Intro to Poetry Prize). His book of translations *I Even Regret Night: Holi Songs of Demerara*, originally published in 1916 (PEN/Heim Translation Fund Grant Award, Kaya Press, 2019).

Faisal Mohyuddin is the author of *The Displaced Children of Displaced Children* (Eyewear Publishing, 2018), which won the 2017 Sexton Prize for Poetry and was a Summer 2018 Recommendation of the Poetry Book Society. Also the author of the chapbook *The Riddle of Longing* (Backbone Press, 2017), he is an educator adviser to the global not-for-profit Narrative 4 and teaches English at Highland Park High School in Illinois.

Feliz Lucia Molina was born and raised in a Filipino diaspora in the San Fernando Valley, California. She holds a BA in Writing & Literature and minor in Religious Studies from Naropa University, and graduate degrees in Literary Arts from Brown University, Clinical Social Work from The University of Chicago, and a PhD (ABD) at the European Graduate School in Switzerland. Her books include *Undercastle* (Magic Helicopter Press), *The Wes Letters* (Outpost19), and *Roulette* forthcoming from Make Now Books. Her chapbooks are *An Essay Of Things About Someone I First Met and Spent Time With For One Day in Tokyo* (Magic Helicopter Press) and *Crystal Marys* (Scary Topiary Press). She is working on a third poetry collection, *Thundercastle*, and a semi-autobiographical screenplay. Her poems are published in and have been commissioned by *PEN America*, *The Poetry Foundation*, *Guggenheim Museum*, *Open Space at SF MOMA*, among others. She can be found at www.felizluciamolina.com.

Sahar Muradi is a NYC-based writer, performer, and educator. She is the author of the chapbook *[G A T E S]* (Black Lawrence Press), co-author of *A Ritual in X Movements* (Montez Press), and co-editor of *One Story, Thirty Stories: An Anthology of Contemporary Afghan American Literature* (University of Arkansas Press). Sahar is a founding member of the Afghan American Artists and Writers Association and has been the recipient of the Stacy Doris Memorial Poetry Award, the Himan Brown Poetry Award, and a Kundiman Poetry Fellowship, among others. She dearly believes in the bottom of the rice pot. www.saharmuradi.com.

Benjamín Naka-Hasebe Kingsley is not the Ben Kingsley best known for his Academy Award-winning role as Mahatma Gandhi. This Ben is a touch less famous, having not acted since his third-grade debut as the Undertaker in *Music Man*. A Kundiman alum, Ben is recipient of the Provincetown FAWC and Tickner Fellowships. He belongs to the Onondaga Nation of Indigenous Americans in New York. His first, second, and third books debut 2018, 2019, and 2020: *Not Your Mama's Melting Pot* (selected by Bob Hicok), *Colonize Me* (Saturnalia), and *Dēmos* forthcoming with Milkweed Editions. Peep his recent work in *Boston Review*, *FIELD*, *jubilat*, *Kenyon Review*, *New England Review*, *Oxford American*, and *Tin House*, among others.

Shankar Narayan is a four-time Pushcart Prize nominee, winner of the 2017 Flyway Sweet Corn Poetry Prize, and has been a fellow at Kundiman and at Hugo House. He is a 4Culture grant recipient for Claiming Space, a project to lift the voices of writers of color, and his chapbook, *Postcards From the New World*, won the Paper Nautilus Debut Series chapbook prize. Shankar draws strength from his global upbringing and from his work as a civil rights attorney for the ACLU. In Seattle, he awakens to the wonders of Cascadia every day, but his heart yearns east to his other hometown, Delhi. Connect with him at shankarnarayan.net.

Matthew Olzmann is the author of two collections of poems, *Mezzanines*, which was selected for the 2011 Kundiman Prize, and *Contradictions in the Design*, both from Alice James Books.

He has been awarded fellowships from the MacDowell Colony, the Kresge Arts Foundation and the Bread Loaf Writers' Conference. His writing has appeared in *Best American Poetry*, *Kenyon Review*, *New England Review*, *Brevity* and elsewhere. He teaches at Dartmouth College and in the MFA Program for Writers at Warren Wilson College.

Shin Yu Pai is the author of *AUX ARCS* (La Alameda, 2013), *Adamantine* (White Pine, 2010), *Sightings* (1913 Press, 2007), and several other books. *ENSO*—a twenty-year survey of her work in poetry, book arts, visual and public art—will be published by Entre Rios Books in March 2020. She has been an artist in residence for Pacific Science Center, Seattle Art Museum, Jack Straw Cultural Center, and Town Hall Seattle. A former Stranger Genius Nominee in Literature, Shin Yu served from 2015 to 2017 as the fourth Poet Laureate of The City of Redmond. She received her MFA from The School of the Art Institute of Chicago and attended the Jack Kerouac School of Disembodied Poetics at Naropa Institute.

Michelle Peñaloza is the author of *Former Possessions of the Spanish Empire*, which won the 2018 Hillary Gravendyk National Poetry Prize (Inlandia Books, 2019). She also wrote two chapbooks, *landscape/heartbreak* (Two Sylvias, 2015), and *Last Night I Dreamt of Volcanoes* (Organic Weapon Arts, 2015). Her poems can be found in *Prairie Schooner*, *Pleiades*, *Third Coast*, *New England Review* and elsewhere. A Kundiman fellow and a graduate of the University of Oregon MFA, Michelle has received fellowships and awards from The Key West Literary Seminar, Oregon Literary Arts, and Artist Trust among many others. Michelle lives in rural Northern California.

Preeti Kaur Rajpal is a poet of the Sikh tradition who grew up in California's San Joaquin Valley. She first began writing as a student of June Jordan's in her Poetry for the People Program. She has been a Fellow with the Loft Literary Center's Mentor Series and Poetry Foundation's Poetry Incubator. She is currently a Jerome Hill Artist Fellow. Her work can be found in *Tupelo Quarterly*, *Spook Mag*, *Lantern Review*, and elsewhere.

Barbara Jane Reyes is the author of *Invocation to Daughters* (City Lights Publishers, 2017). She was born in Manila, Philippines, raised in the San Francisco Bay Area, and is the author of four previous collections of poetry, *Gravities of Center* (Arkipelago Books, 2003), *Poeta en San Francisco* (Tinfish Press, 2005), which received the James Laughlin Award of the Academy of American Poets, *Diwata* (BOA Editions, Ltd., 2010), which received the Global Filipino Literary Award for Poetry, and *To Love as Aswang* (Philippine American Writers and Artists, Inc., 2015). She is also the author of the chapbooks *Easter Sunday* (Ypolita Press, 2008) *Cherry* (Portable Press at Yo-Yo Labs, 2008), and *For the City that Nearly Broke Me* (Aztlán Libre Press, 2012). Her sixth book, *Letters to a Young Brown Girl*, is forthcoming from BOA Editions, Ltd. in 2020.

Karen Rigby is the author of *Chinoiserie* (Ahsahta Press, 2012) and two chapbooks. Her poems have been published in *The London Magazine*, *Palette Poetry*, and other journals. She lives in Arizona. www.karenrigby.com

Brynn Saito is a poet, educator, and organizer. She is the author of two books of poetry from Red Hen Press, *Power Made Us Swoon* (2016) and *The Palace of Contemplating Departure* (2013), winner of the Benjamin Saltman Award and a finalist for the Northern California Book Award. She also co-authored, with Traci Brimhall, the chapbook *Bright Power, Dark Peace* (Diode Editions, 2016). Brynn is an Assistant Professor of Creative Writing in the English Department at California State University, Fresno.

Craig Santos Perez is a native Chamorro from the Pacific Island of Guam. He is author of four books of poetry and the editor of four anthologies of Pacific literature. He is an associate professor in the English department at the University of Hawai'i, Manoa.

Vijay Seshadri the author of the poetry books *Wild Kingdom*, *The Long Meadow*, and *3 Sections*, as well as many essays, reviews, and memoir fragments. His work has been widely published and anthologized and recognized with many honors, most recently the 2014 Pulitzer Prize for Poetry and, in 2015, the

Literature Award of the American Academy of Arts and Letters. He currently teaches at Sarah Lawrence College and is the poetry editor of *The Paris Review*.

Purvi Shah inspires change as a non-profit consultant and writer. During the 10th anniversary of 9/11, she directed *Together We Are New York*, a community-based poetry project highlighting Asian American voices. For her leadership fighting violence against women, she won the inaugural SONY South Asian Social Service Excellence Award. *Terrain Tracks*, her debut collection on migration and belonging, won the Many Voices Project prize. Her new book, *Miracle Marks*, explores women and the sacred. She serves as a board member of The Poetry Project. Her favorite art practices are her sparkly eyeshadow and raucous laughter. Discover more @PurviPoets or www.purvipoets.net.

Sun Yung Shin, MFA, MAT, is the author of poetry/essay collections *Unbearable Splendor* (Minnesota Book Award); *Rough, and Savage*; and *Skirt Full of Black* (Asian American Literary Award) (all published by Coffee House Press). She is the editor of *A Good Time for the Truth: Race in Minnesota* and co-editor of *Outsiders Within: Writing on Transracial Adoption*. Her bilingual (Korean/English) illustrated children's book is *Cooper's Lesson*. She is the co-director of Poetry Asylum and is a healing practitioner (biodynamic craniosacral therapy and Reiki). She lives in Minneapolis; more at www.sunyungshin.com.

Monica Sok is a Cambodian American poet and the daughter of former refugees. She is the author of *A Nail the Evening Hangs On* and her work has been recognized with a Discovery Prize from the 92nd Street Y Unterberg Poetry Center. She is the recipient of fellowships from Hedgebrook, the Elizabeth George Foundation, the National Endowment for the Arts, Kundiman, Jerome Foundation, MacDowell Colony, Saltonstall Foundation for the Arts, and others. Currently, Sok is a 2018-2020 Wallace Stegner Fellow at Stanford University and also teaches poetry at the Center for Empowering Refugees and Immigrants and Banteay Srei in Oakland. She is originally from Lancaster, Pennsylvania.

Sofia M. Starnes, born in Manila, Philippines, and a US citizen since 1989, served as Virginia Poet Laureate (2012-2014). She is the author of six poetry collections, most recently *The Consequence of Moonlight* (Paraclete Press, 2018), and the recipient of numerous awards, including a Poetry Fellowship from the Virginia Commission for the Arts, five Pushcart Prize nominations, and an honorary Doctor of Letters degree from Union College (KY). Sofia was Poetry Editor of *The Anglican Theological Review* from 2007 to 2019. She has been a translator for Galería Cayón (Madrid, Spain), the Ayala Foundation (Manila, Philippines), and Iberdrola (Bilbao, Spain). She lives in Williamsburg, Virginia, with her husband, Bill.

Eileen R. Tabios has released over 60 collections of poetry, fiction, essays, and experimental biographies from publishers in ten countries. Books include five Selected Poems based on poetry forms: the tercet, visual poetry, the catalog or list poem, the prose poem, and the hay(na)ku. Her award-winning body of work includes invention of the hay(na)ku poetic form and a first poetry book, *Beyond Life Sentences*, that received the Philippines' National Book Award for Poetry. She has received recognition through awards, grants and residencies. More information is available at www.eileenrtabios.com.

Adeeba Shahid Talukder is a Pakistani American poet, singer, and translator of Urdu and Persian poetry. She is the author of *What Is Not Beautiful* (Glass Poetry Press, 2018) and her book *Shahr-e-jaanaan: The City of the Beloved* (Tupelo Press, 2020), was awarded the Kundiman Poetry Prize. Her poetry has appeared in *Poem-A-Day, Gulf Coast, Meridian, The Margins, Best American Poetry,* and elsewhere. A Best of the Net finalist and Pushcart nominee, Adeeba holds an MFA in Creative Writing from the University of Michigan and a 2017 Emerging Poets Fellowship from Poets House.

Amy Uyematsu is a sansei poet and teacher from Los Angeles. She has five published collections: *Basic Vocabulary, The Yellow Door, Stone Bow Prayer, Nights of Fire, Nights of Rain,* and *30 Miles* *from J-Town*. Amy was co-editor of the widely used anthology, *Roots: An Asian American Reader* (UCLA Asian American Studies Center, 1971). She currently teaches a writing workshop at the Far East Lounge in LA's Little Tokyo.

Ocean Vuong is the author of novel *On Earth We're Briefly Gorgeous* (Penguin Press, 2019) and the poetry collection *Night Sky with Exit Wounds*, which was a *New York Times* Top 10 Book of 2016 and winner of the T.S. Eliot Prize and Forward Prize for Best First Collection. His writings have been featured in *The Atlantic, The Nation, The New Yorker, The New York Times*, and *American Poetry Review*. Born in Saigon, Vietnam, he currently lives in Western Massachusetts where he serves as an Assistant Professor in the MFA Program for Poets and Writers at Umass-Amherst.

Jane Wong's poems can be found in *Best American Poetry 2015, POETRY, American Poetry Review, Third Coast, AGNI*, and others. A Kundiman fellow, she is the recipient of a Pushcart Prize and fellowships from the U.S. Fulbright Program, the Fine Arts Work Center, Hedgebrook, Artist Trust, and Bread Loaf. She is the author of *Overpour* (Action Books, 2016) and *How to Not Be Afraid of Everything* (Alice James, forthcoming). She is an Assistant Professor of Creative Writing at Western Washington University.

Bryan Thao Worra is the Lao Minnesotan Poet Laureate. The author of 8+ books, he is a 2009 US National Endowment for the Arts Fellow and a 2019 Joyce Award recipient. The Creative Works Editor for the *Journal of Southeast Asian American Education and Advancement,* he is the president of a 40-year old international speculative poetry association. In 2012, he represented the nation of Laos as its Cultural Olympian during the London Summer Games. www.thaoworra.com.

Khaty Xiong is the author of *Poor Anima* (Apogee Press, 2015), which holds the distinction of being the first full-length collection of poetry published by a Hmong American woman in the United States. Her work has been featured in *Poetry*, the *New York Times, How Do I Begin?: A Hmong American Literary Anthology* (Heyday, 2011), and elsewhere. She's been awarded grants and fellowships from Vermont Studio Center (2020), Jack Jones Literary Arts (2019), The MacDowell Colony (2017), and the Ohio Arts Council (2016).

ACKNOWLEDGMENTS

Neil Aitken. "The Art of Forgetting," "How We Are Saved," and "Prodigal." From *The Lost Country of Sight*. Copyright © 2008 by Neil Aitken. Reprinted by permission of Anhinga Press. Unauthorized duplication not permitted.

Kaveh Akbar. "Despite My Efforts Even My Prayers Have Turned into Threats." Copyright © by Kaveh Akbar. Originally published in *Poetry Magazine* (November 2016). Reprinted by permission of the author.

Kazim Ali. "Divination" and "Cover Me" Copyright © by Kazim Ali. Originally published in *Fiddlehead Journal* (Issue 279, Spring 2019). Reprinted by permission of the author.

Marci Calabretta Cancio-Bello. "Invocation." From *The Hour of the Ox*. Copyright © 2016 by Marci Calabretta Cancio-Bello. Reprinted by permission of the University of Pittsburgh Press.

Marianne Chan. "Origin Story" Copyright © by Marianne Chan. Originally published in *BOAAT* (November/December 2016). Reprinted by permission of the author. "December 1998." Copyright © by Marianne Chan. Originally published in *West Branch* (Spring/Summer 2018 issue, Number 87). Reprinted by permission of the author.

K-Ming Chang. "Televangelism" and "Reincarnation." From *Past Lives, Future Bodies*. Copyright © 2018 by K-Ming Chang. Reprinted by permission of Black Lawrence Press.

Tina Chang. "Mankind is So Fallible." From *Hybrida*. Copyright © 2019 Tina Chang. Reprinted by permission of W.W. Norton & Company. "Ascension," "The Burning," and "Easter" from *Half-Lit Houses*. Copyright © 2004 by Tina Chang. Reprinted with the permission of The Permissions Company, LLC on behalf of Four Way Books, www.fourwaybooks.com.

Acknowledgments

Jennifer S. Cheng. *"from* Dear Blank Space." Copyright © by Jennifer S. Cheng. Originally published in *Entropy* (December 31, 2015). Reprinted by permission of the author.

Wendy Chin-Tanner. "Advent." From *Anyone Will Tell You.* Copyright © 2019 Wendy Chin-Tanner. Reprinted by permission of Sibling Rivalry Press.

Rachelle Cruz. "How to Pray." From *God's Will For Monsters.* Copyright © 2017 Rachelle Cruz. Reprinted by permission of Inlandia Institute.

Debra Kang Dean. "Adam's Apple." From *Precipitates*. Copyright © 2003 by Debra Kang Dean. Reprinted with the permission of The Permissions Company, LLC on behalf of BOA Editions, Ltd., www.boaeditions.org.

Christian Detisch. "Conversion." Copyright © 2020 by Christian Detisch.

Oliver de la Paz. "Dear Empire," and "Dear Empire." From *Post Subject: A Fable.* Copyright © 2014 by Oliver de la Paz. Reprinted by permission of The University of Akron Press. "Aubade with Constellations, Some Horses, and Snow." From *Furious Lullaby*. Copyright © 2007 by Oliver de la Paz. Reprinted by permission of Southern Illinois University Press.

Duy Doan. "Prayer in Writing" and "Allegory for Family Members." From *We Play a Game*. Copyright © 2018 by Duy Doan. Reprinted by permission of Yale University Press.

Christy NaMee Eriksen. "Congee" Copyright © 2020 by Christy NaMee Eriksen.

Tarfia Faizullah. "Acolyte." From *Registers of Illuminated Villages*. Copyright © 2018 by Tarfia Faizullah. Reprinted with the permission of The Permissions Company, LLC, on behalf of Graywolf Press, Minneapolis, Minnesota, www.graywolfpress.

Acknowledgments

org. "Reading Celan at the Liberation War Museum." From *Seam*. Copyright © 2014 by Tarfia Faizullah. Reprinted by permission of Southern Illinois University Press.

Sarah Gambito. "Old Dominion" and "Virginia". From *Loves You*. Copyright © 2019 by Sarah Gambito. Reprinted with the permission of Persea Books, Inc. (New York), www.perseabooks.com. All rights reserved.

Kathleen Hellen. "The Way of Tea." Copyright © Kathleen Hellen. Originally published in *Poetry International* (Issue 9). Reprinted with the permission of the author.

Leslieann Hobayan. "Dear Home." Copyright © by Leslieann Hobayan. Originally published in *Asteri(x) Journal* (May 2018). Reprinted with the permission of the author.

Su Hwang. "When Streets Are Paved With Gold." Copyright © by Su Hwang. Originally published in *wildness journal* (Issue 15, Summer 2018). "Cancer." Copyright © by Su Hwang. Originally published in *Tinderbox Poetry Journal* (Vol. 4, Issue 2, March 2017). Reprinted with permission of the author.

W. Todd Kaneko. "Atheism," "Faith," and "Disbelief." Copyright © 2020 by W. Todd Kaneko.

Vandana Khanna. "Blue Madonna," page 37 "Elephant God," page 40. From *Train to Agra*. Copyright © 2001 by Vandana Khanna. Reprinted by permission of Southern Illinois University Press. "Hindu Mythology in Shorthand." Copyright © by Vandana Khanna. Originally published in *Prairie Schooner* (Volume 89, Number 1, Spring 2015) "Prayer to Recognize the Body." From *The Goddess Monologues*. Copyright © 2016 by Vandana Khanna. Reprinted with permission of Diode Editions.

Hei Kyong Kim. "Water Mask." Copyright © 2020 by Hei Kyong Kim.

Acknowledgments

Benjamín Naka-Hasebe Kingsley. "Jesus in a Jar of Mayonnaise." From *Not Your Mama's Melting Pot*. Copyright © 2018 by Benjamín Naka-Hasebe Kinglsey. Reprinted with permission of The Backwaters Press.

E. J. Koh. "Shaman," "Father in His Old Age," "The Mountain" and "Floaters." From *A Lesser Love*. Copyright © 2017 by E. J. Koh. Reprinted with permission of Pleiades Press.

Hyejung Kook. "A Consolation: Permitting Mourning." Copyright © by Hyejung Kook. Originally published in *Prairie Schooner* (Volume 92, Number 1, Spring 2018). "Invention No. 9 in f minor." Copyright © by Hyejung Kook. Originally published in *The Indianapolis Review* (Issue 4: Spring 2018). Reprinted with permission of the author.

Jennifer Kwon Dobbs. "How to Eat Your Love" and "Elegy for a Song Between." From *Interrogation Room*. Copyright © 2018 by Jennifer Kwon Dobbs. Reprinted with the permission of The Permissions Company, LLC on behalf of behalf of White Pine Press, www.whitepine.org.

Ed Bok Lee. "Box of Personal Gods" and "Random Floating Cells with Style." From *Mitochondrial Night*. Copyright © 2018 by Ed Bok Lee. Reprinted with permission from Coffee House Press.

Li-Young Lee. "Arise, Go Down" and "The City in Which I Love You." From *The City in Which I Love You*. Copyright © 1990 by Li-Young Lee. Reprinted with the permission of The Permissions Company, LLC on behalf of BOA Editions, Ltd., www.boaeditions.org. "Cuckoo Flower on the Witness Stand," "Have You Prayed," from *BEHIND MY EYES* by Li-Young Lee. Copyright © 2008 by Li-Young Lee. Used by permission of W. W. Norton & Company, Inc.

Joseph O. Legaspi. "Easter, Bonifacio High Street." Copyright © by Joseph O. Legaspi. Originally published in *The Common: A Modern Sense of Place* (Issue 16). "Grace." Copyright © by Joseph

O. Legaspi. Originally published in *New England Review* (Issue 37.4). "Sketches from a Childhood Sea." Copyright © Joseph O. Legaspi. Originally published in *Memorius* (Issue 26) and reprinted in *Best of the Net* 2016. Reprinted with permission of the author.

Eugenia Leigh. "Psalm 107" and "Selah." From *Blood, Sparrows and Sparrows*. Copyright © 2014. Reprinted with the permission of The Permissions Company, LLC on behalf of Four Way Books, www.fourwaybooks.com. "What I Miss Most About Hell," Copyright © by Eugenia Leigh. Originally published in *Waxwing* (Issue XII, Summer 2017). Reprinted with permission of the author.

Kenji C. Liu. "Migratory Daughter." From *Map of an Onion*. Copyright © 2016 by Kenji C. Liu. Published with permission of Inlandia Institute. Reprinted with permission of the author.

Timothy Liu. "Love Poem in a Steam Room Run by Sufis" and "Transcendence." Copyright © 2020 by Timothy Liu.

Shireen Madon. "Religion." Copyright © by Shireen Madon. Originally published in *Prairie Schooner* (Fall 2017, Volume 91, Number 3). Reprinted with permission of the author.

Mia Ayumi Malhotra. "The Losing Begins," "One Day You'll Look in the Mirror and See Lions," and "To My Many Mothers, Issel and Nisei". From *Isako Isako*. Copyright © 2017, 2018 by Mia Ayumi Malhotra. Reprinted with the permission of The Permissions Company LLC on behalf of Alice James Books, www.alicejamesbooks.org.

Vikas Menon. "Prayer for the Rending" and "Samadhi." Copyright © 2020 by Vikas Menon.

Rajiv Mohabir. "Whale Story." Copyright © by Rajiv Mohabir. Originally published in *Hawai'i Review* (Issue 81). Reprinted with permission of the author.

Faisal Mohyuddin. "The Opening," "In Defense of Monsters,"

and "Ghazal for the Lost." From *The Displaced Children of Displaced Children*. Copyright © 2018 by Faisal Mohyuddin. Reprinted with permission of Eyewear Publishing, Ltd.

Feliz Lucia Molina. "Hello Kitty Virgin Mary." Originally published in *PoetryNow* (2018). Reprinted with permission of the author.

Sahar Muradi. "Timbuktu." From *[G A T E S]*. Copyright © 2017 by Sahar Muradi. Reprinted with permission of Black Lawrence Press.

Shankar Narayan. "Three-Spirit Prayer Before the Tandav" and "Invocation for the Impossible Present." Copyright © 2020 by Shankar Narayan. "Psalm from the Old World." Originally published in Really System (Issue Fourteen, Spring 2017). Reprinted with permission of the author.

Matthew Olzmann. "Prayer Near a Farm by Black Mountain, North Carolina: 11:36 pm, Early May," and "Nate Brown Looking for a Moose." From *Contradictions in the Design*. Copyright © 2016 by Matthew Olzmann. Reprinted with the permission of The Permissions Company, LLC on behalf of Alice James Books www.alicejamesbooks.org. "Letter to a Bridge Made of Rope—." Copyright © by Matthew Olzmann. Originally published in *Inch #27*, Bull City Press (Winter 2014). Reprinted with permission of the author.

Shin Yu Pai. "Burning Monk." From *Adamantine*. Copyright © 2010 by Shin Yu Pai. Reprinted with the permission of The Permissions Company, LLC on behalf of behalf of White Pine Press, www.whitepine.org. "Easter Sunday." From *Aux Arcs*. Copyright © 2013 by Shin Yu Pai. Reprinted with permission of La Alameda.

Michelle Peñaloza. "Thread Rite." Copyright © by Michelle Peñaloza. Originally published in *Bellingham Review* (Spring/ Summer 2012). "Vestige." Copyright © by Michelle Peñaloza. Originally published in *Lantern Review* (#2 Winter 2011). Reprinted with permission of the author.

Preeti Kaur Rajpal. "dirge after oak creek" and "making roti in the langar kitchen off highway 99." Copyright © 2020 by Preeti Kaur Rajpal.

Barbara Jane Reyes. "The Gospel of Juana de la Cruz" and "Psalm for Mary Jane Veloso." From *Invocation to Daughters*. Copyright © 2017 by Barbara Jane Reyes. Reprinted with the permission of The Permissions Company LLC on behalf of City Lights Books, www.citylights.com. "In the City, a New Congregation Finds Her." From *Diwata*. Copyright © 2010 by Barbara Janes Reyes. Reprinted with the permission of The Permissions Company LLC on behalf of BOA Editions, Ltd., www.boaeditions.org. "[galleon prayer]." From *Poeta en San Francisco*. Copyright © 2005 Barbara Jane Reyes. Reprinted with permission from TinFish Press.

Karen Rigby. "The Story of Adam and Eve" and "Cebolla Church." From *Chinoiserie*, copyright © 2011 by Karen Rigby and *Savage Machinery*, copyright © 2008 by Karen Rigby. Reprinted with permission of Ahsahta Press and Finishing Line Press.

Brynn Saito. "How to Prepare the Mind for Lightning." Copyright © by Brynn Saito. Originally published in Poets.org "Poem-a-Day" (2016). "Afterlife," "Reincarnation," and "Shadow and Release." Copyright © 2020 by Brynn Saito.

Craig Santos Perez. "(dear fu'una)," "(dear puntan)," and "(dear fu'una)." From *unincorporated territory [lukao]*. Copyright © 2017 Craig Santos Perez. Reprinted with permission from Omnidawn. "Patron Saint of Bingo." Copyright © 2020 by Craig Santos Perez.

Vijay Seshadri. "The Long Meadow" and "Imaginary Number." From *The Long Meadow*. Copyright © 2004 by Vijay Seshadri. Reprinted with the permission of The Permissions Company, Inc., on behalf of Graywolf Press, www.graywolfpress.org.

Purvi Shah. "In the 21st century, Mira remarks — Krishna's

ways of loving belong in a parallel universe," "Beating her soiled clothes, Saraswati reaches God and bursts into tears," "At the edge of her bangle, Saraswati reckons with the one flame." and From *Miracle Marks*. Copyright © 2019 by Purvi Shah. Published 2019 by Curbstone Books / Northwestern University Press. All rights reserved.

Sun Yung Shin. "Papaver Somniferum" and "Names Between the Holes | Lacing the Dead Father." Copyright © 2020 by Sun Yung Shin.

Monica Sok. "Song of an Orphaned Soldier Clearing Land Mines." From *A Nail the Evening Hangs On*. Originally published by *TriQuarterly* 149 (Winter/Spring 2016). Copyright © 2016, 2020 by Monica Sok. Reprinted with the permission of The Permissions Company, LLC on behalf of Copper Canyon Press www.coppercanyonpress.org.

Sofia M. Starnes. "Baptism of Desire." From *The Consequence of Moonlight: Poems*. Copyright © 2018 by Sofia M. Starnes. Reprinted with permission of Paraclete Press. "Nightlife." From *Fully Into Ashes*. Copyright © 2011 by Sofia M. Starnes. Reprinted with permission of Wings Press.

Eileen R. Tabios. "The Secret Life of an Angel" and "Maganda Begins." From *The In(ter)vention of the Hay(na)ku: Selected Tercets 1996–2019*. Copyright © 2019 by Eileen R. Tabios. Reprinted with permission of Marsh Hawk Press.

Adeeba Shahid Talukder. "Clot," "God," and "On Beauty" from *Shahr-e-jaanaan: The City of The Beloved*. Copyright © 2019 by Adeeba Shahid Talukder. Reprinted with the permission of The Permissions Company, LLC, on behalf of Tupelo Press, www.tupelopress.org.

Amy Uyematsu. "Pilgrimage to Jokhang Temple" and "Zap #30." From *Basic Vocabulary*. Copyright © 2016 Amy Uyematsu. Reprinted with permission of Red Hen Press. "The Older, The

ABOUT THE EDITORS

Leah Silvieus was born in South Korea and adopted to the U.S. at three months of age. She spent her early childhood and adolescence in small towns in Montana's Bitterroot Valley and western Colorado. The author of a full-length poetry collection, *Arabilis*, and two chapbooks, *Anemochory* and *Season of Dares*, Silvieus is a recipient of awards from The Academy of American Poets and The Fulbright Program. She serves on Kundiman's Junior Board and as a mentor on The Brooklyn Poets Bridge.

Lee Herrick is the author of three books of poems, *Scar and Flower, Gardening Secrets of the Dead*, and *This Many Miles from Desire*. He served as Fresno Poet Laureate from 2015–2017. Herrick was born in Daejeon, South Korea, adopted at ten months old, and raised in California. He teaches at Fresno City College and in the MFA Program at Sierra Nevada College.

ABOUT ORISON BOOKS

Orison Books is a 501(c)3 non-profit literary press focused on the life of the spirit from a broad and inclusive range of perspectives. We seek to publish books of exceptional poetry, fiction, and non-fiction from perspectives spanning the spectrum of spiritual and religious thought, ethnicity, gender identity, and sexual orientation.

As a non-profit literary press, Orison Books depends on the support of donors. To find out more about our mission and our books, or to make a donation, please visit www.orisonbooks.com.